Impact

Impact

Personal Portraits of Activism

Edited by Michelle Duster and Trina Sotira

*Muse*Write
PRESS

Copyright © 2020 by MuseWrite Press
P. O. Box 19550, Chicago, IL 60619, USA
www.musewrite.com

Library of Congress Cataloging-in-Publication Data available upon request.
ISBN 978-0-9899609-3-9

Cover design by Robin Ludwig Designs
Copy Editor: Crystal Fencke
Formatting: Polgarus Studio

To all who refuse to stay silent in the face of injustice, you make a difference in your own way.
- Michelle Duster

For those who hope, like me, that there is a way out of the hate and hurt.
-Trina Sotira

CONTENTS

FOREWORD   xiii
Michelle Duster

RACIAL JUSTICE

AN UNNAMED VOICE FOR CHANGE   3
Clara B. Freeman

BREATHING IN AMERICA   8
Annette M. Alston

READING INVISIBLE MAN   14
Marianne Taylor

A COLORIST IN RECOVERY   16
Stephanie J. Gates

THE CONFINEMENT CAGE   21
Erin Goseer Mitchell

ANY OTHER NAME   24
Brian C. Billings

SOCIAL JUSTICE

I GAVE PEACE A CHANCE   37
Terri Elders

QUIET ACTIVIST   41
Susan M. Winstead

#StandOnEveryCorner   44
Rita Moe

GAVAGE   47
Richard Downing

BEYOND CASSEROLES   49
Judy Seldin-Cohen

THE THORN   54
Dee Allen.

ADD A LITTLE COLOR FOR JUSTICE   58
Sandra Hall

PATHWAYS   64
Jarrett Mazza

AFTER THE ELECTION   69
Allene Nichols

POEM TO MY BROTHER, JOSE BELLO   71
A. J. Chilson

GENDER EQUITY JUSTICE

I THINK OF LYN LIFSHIN   75
Laura Sweeney

HOOKED   77
Anne Farrer Scott

THE BIRTH OF HEALING AND ACTIVISM   81
Greta McClain

STANDING LONG ENOUGH TO MOURN   86
Hunter Liguore

WOMEN   90
Anjana Satpathy

BLUE, PINK, AND WHITE STRIPES   93
Aila Alvina Boyd

HEALTHCARE JUSTICE

BRENDA'S PLAN   99
Uzomah Ugwu

I HAVE NOT FORGOTTEN HOW TO FIGHT   102
Carole Ann Moleti

SILENCES: ROE VS. WADE   110
Patti Capel Swartz

MAKING STRIDES WITH EVERY STEP   116
Lisa Braxton

AT THE PAIN CLINIC   120
Terry Sanville

NATURAL NEIGHBORHOOD   123
Keith A. Raymond

ENVIRONMENTAL JUSTICE

EARTH IS GOD   127
Naida Mujkic

WHY I BECAME AN ACTIVIST   129
Judy Hogan

**HOW BECOMING A GRANDMOTHER
TURNED ME INTO AN ACTIVIST**   132
Alexandra Grabbe

MAKING A DIFFERENCE BY IMPLEMENTING
IMPORTANT PUBLIC PROJECTS   135
Leslie Penelope Recht

NOT ALL GUNS BLAZING   140
Gerard Sarnat

EDUCATIONAL JUSTICE

DAY ONE   143
Jacqueline Ruegg

LETTER TO C & T   145
Linda L. Elman

WHY DOES IT HURT SO MUCH?   148
Deirdre L. Clawson

THEY DON'T SEE US   153
Sharron Goodman-Hill

PUNCHING BAG   158
Chad W. Lutz

THE BODY OF THE ESSAY   159
CMarie Fuhrman

REPRESENTATION IN PUBLICATION   165
Leah Olajide

THE FIGHT AGAINST STEREOTYPES   168
Jennifer Brown Banks

TO BE SEEN AND HEARD   170
Tony Bradburn

ASHLEY JUDD GOES TO COLLEGE AT AGE 49   175
Laura Sweeney

ACTIVISM   177
Unique Shaw-Smith and Chantae Still

MORE THAN MERELY KNOW   180
Marion Deutsche Cohen

⊿⊿⊿

AFTERWORD   181
Trina Sotira

CONTRIBUTORS   183

EDITORS   193

DISCUSSION QUESTIONS   195

FOREWORD

Michelle Duster

When many people think of activism, the first thing that comes to mind is protestors who are in the streets. For this reason, some people do not think of themselves as activists because they are quietly working in spaces that are not in direct contact with police. They are not using bullhorns, yelling chants, or getting tear-gassed or arrested. They are organizing letter-writing campaigns or petitions. They are creating programs in institutions. They are opening their institutions to support those in need. They are meeting with politicians. They are working phone banks. They are creating literary pieces, music, theater, film, and other works that challenge mainstream narratives. They are creating programs, changing curriculum, impacting policies, working with students to help them combat some of the challenges of the world. They work on committees, with religious groups, neighbors, youth groups, media outlets, and organizations to impact change.

Speaking up and challenging systems is not easy. There is always the danger of being labeled a troublemaker, difficult, and/or disgruntled, among other names. Even though the saying goes, "The squeaky wheel gets the grease," we all know, sometimes the squeaky wheel gets replaced or ostracized or marginalized. Sometimes people can face great danger when they challenge the status quo. And that danger does not have to be extreme as in the form of physical violence. It can be the danger of losing a job or being isolated from a social group or community.

It takes courage to be one of the few who dare to say something, in written, verbal, or action form. Those around you might not understand your convictions and sometimes it takes a leap of faith and internal fortitude to fight for something others cannot see or speak about something others cannot hear.

Historically, major societal transformation has happened because of demands from the bottom up versus the top down.

Those in power usually need to be pressured to move into a direction that is fair and equitable. The fight for change is usually fraught with struggle. There is resistance. There are attempts to silence or discredit. It can be challenging to stay hopeful. It takes strength to keep fighting against what can seem like insurmountable odds. But we need to stay encouraged and believe that struggle is part of the process of change. As Frederick Douglass famously said:

> If there is no struggle there is no progress. Those who profess to favor freedom and yet deprecate agitation, are men who want crops without plowing up the ground, they want rain without thunder and lightning. They want the ocean without the awful roar of its many waters. This struggle may be a moral one, or it may be a physical one, and it may be both moral and physical, but it must be a struggle. Power concedes nothing without a demand. It never did and never will.

Throughout the history of the United States, major transformations have occurred due to the hard work of activists. Women gained the right to vote through a sustained campaign of activism over several decades. For over 150 post-slavery years, African Americans have sustained incredible resistance and activism in the fight for equality in almost every area of life including education, housing, voting rights, land ownership, and policing. Brown people have had long histories of struggle with activism being key to progress. One of the more famous struggles for Hispanics is that of farm workers, led by Cesar Chavez and Dolores Huerta fighting for better working conditions. Native Americans have more recently resisted the building of the Dakota Access Pipeline and continued resistance against racially offensive names of professional sports leagues. Every country has examples of groups that have faced their own struggles and there have always been those who fought to make change.

Although there has always been tension between various political parties, ethnic and religious groups, economic classes, and regional areas, the first few years after the 2016 United States' presidential election has brought many tensions to the surface and exploded into mass and visible resistance. From the 2017 Women's March (the largest march across the globe in history) to 2020 marches and protests after the murder of several unarmed Black people including George Floyd, there has been an uptick in public protests.

People marching in the streets is what leads headlines. However, the behind-the-scenes work is just as important and equally effective. The goal of *Impact: Personal Portraits of Activism* is to showcase and celebrate the quiet and sometimes solo forms of activism. Because it all matters. Every act of speaking out against oppression, injustice, inequality, and disparity matters.

The essays, poems, short stories, and play featured in this collection are portraits of activism that address racial, social, gender equity, healthcare, environmental, and education justice. My great-grandmother, Ida B. Wells, was a journalist, civil rights activist, and suffragist who spent her life fighting for justice and equality. As she once said, "The way to right wrongs is to turn the light of truth upon them." So, the first step toward change is helping people understand what the problem is. Then, work to create and implement solutions in the form of changing laws, policies, businesses, and institutions.

As we all live through and engage in this transformational time in our history, the contributors to *Impact* will continue to inspire those they work with in person, but also those who read this book that they may never meet. These changemakers provide examples for how everyone can make a difference where they are. We can all learn from each other and work in our own ways to make this world more equal and just for all.

RACIAL JUSTICE

AN UNNAMED VOICE FOR CHANGE

Clara B. Freeman

Growing up in the Mississippi Delta in the 1950s and 60s during the Jim Crow era, my parents, like many people of color, lived in the country and worked on the farms of white folks. As a child, my siblings and I never knew any differently. We went about our young lives happily enjoying the ambiance of nature's countryside. There was never a lack of wide-open spaces to pique our interest or stymie our energy. Coming of age in the country, I ran about with other kids, on the farm, freely and naively, unknowingly sequestered from what was happening in the South and in the rest of the world. Racial unrest and separation between the races were a growing concern that, as children, we knew very little about. Our family, along with other Black families lived in this close-knit bubble consisting of hard work, school, church and weekend playdays, offset by the ambiance of Mother Nature.

I loved the outdoors, playing with other children and running amuck on expansive farmlands of green pastures where cows and horses grazed, haystacks to play hide-and-seek in, cotton fields, pecan groves, apple and persimmon trees. Sometimes on weekends, a group of us kids romped about neighboring vegetable gardens to crack open ripe watermelons, eating the yellow hearts of the melon as its sweet juices ran down our fingers. These gardens planted by Black mothers supplemented their families with a much-needed food source during harsh Mississippi winters that often prevented the men from working. We lived a simple lifestyle. Eventually, I grew to the realization that Black people's skin color was a deterrent to our being treated equally.

Around the age of eleven, living in the bowels of a racist Mississippi Delta, something in me began to change. An increasing awareness started an explosion in my entire being that would topple my pristine fantasies and offer me a gigantic push into reality. I couldn't even fathom the word "activist" in my need to right this wrong in a young brain that was witnessing such inequality between the races. We were supposedly living equal but separate, and even that was a lie. Looking around with newly open eyes, I realized that Black people were indeed living separate from white people, but not equally in the least.

Black people couldn't drink from the fountain of white people in the small town of Drew. Couldn't swim in certain specified "whites only" pools. There were signs indicating stores that catered only to whites and schools remained segregated until 1970 when I became a high school freshman. Even though Black kids and white kids were attending the same school, governed by the passing of the Civil Rights Act of 1964, Black people were still treated as less than. It was maybe a year after integration that many white parents removed their children from public schools, enrolling them in private Sunflower "Academies" using funding allotted by the state to do so.

Growing up, my older sister, Bill, was my idol. She was pretty and smart and funny. When Bill was in her late teens, she challenged authority. One Saturday afternoon, she and some of our cousins went exploring on the farm's private lake and were promptly caught in the act. Blustering with anger, the owner hastily drove his little two-seater Jeep up to our house to tell our parents what my sister and cousins had done. Bill got the whipping of her life from mama that day. I remember feeling sad for her and angry that mama would whip her for what seemed like such a trivial thing. At the same time, my heart swelled with pride for how she and my cousins had brazenly traipsed through that lakeside cabin and defied one of the white man's rules.

Watching how my daddy was paid for his hard work and having to wait for hours after to get paid was another private torture for me. The men on that farm would have been working from sunup to sundown Monday through Friday and on Saturday mornings, but had to wait well into Saturday afternoons for their pay, which was in cash. I've since discovered over the years how this maneuver was just a clever way for the landowner to avoid paying taxes. Of course, no person on that farm questioned the "white man's schemes," simply because they didn't know about wages and taxes and refunds from the IRS.

Daddy and the other men were efficient and skilled farm

laborers. They didn't know about the workings of economics because, like daddy, they never finished school or, never even attended school. The fact that they were treated as simple farmhands didn't escape me. The straw that broke the camel's back came when mama took me to the country store one balmy Saturday evening. The young white boy behind the counter couldn't have been older than fifteen. Maybe he was put there to help him pass the time. After the kid rang up mama's supplies, he asked if there was anything else she needed.

Mama responded, "No Sir." Hearing my strong, wonderful mama, say "sir," sent me into a tailspin of a mountainous and dark fury, of which I had never experienced before.

"Mama, you don't have to say, "yes sir" to him. "He's just a boy!" Mama was silent as she retrieved her purchases. She remained quiet when she took me by the shoulders and steered me out of the store. It's only since I became an adult that I can recognize and reflect on all that Black people had to endure, from slavery, to terrorism from the KKK, to the 50s and 60s Jim Crow in the South; how their life experiences could lead to some form of docility as a measure of protection for themselves and their families. I was brash and young and hot tempered and never stopped to stop to think about how my parents and other Black folks' reticence might have contributed to their survival.

I have participated in two sit-ins in my life. The most memorable was after the murder of a popular senior who was valedictorian of her class. Just hours after she delivered her graduation speech, Jo Etha Collier was shot three times in the abdomen by three white men. She was standing on a corner in uptown Drew, waiting for a friend to walk her home. She still had her cap and gown on.

Those racists had taken a joy ride, out looking for trouble and had found and acted on their hate by killing a bright beacon of light. It was devastating to her family, to my brother who was her classmate, to the Black community and entire nation. There was a sit-in at the school, where Black and white students sat on the lawn of the high school in protest. I was also part of a group of Black protestors, who rode with friends who had cars to the courthouse in Greenville, Mississippi to hear the verdict of these white murderers. The trial was brief, and those men were blatantly and quickly acquitted.

5

I was naive in so many ways, perhaps due in part to having been raised in the country. Maybe it was also because of how I was raised. Born into a family of ten brothers and sisters, having a mama and daddy who didn't talk about race or our rights as a people, I struggled for understanding. Luckily, a friend's parents, who were more proactive in fighting for the rights of Black folks, allowed me to tag along to meetings in the homes of people they knew. Unbeknownst to me at the time, another friend's mother was an activist and celebrity in the town. Mrs. Mae Bertha Carter was one of the founding members of Mississippi activists fighting diligently for Black people's civil rights. She welcomed many famous civil rights activists in her home. This was the first woman of color in Drew, Mississippi to send her children to a segregated school. I met Mrs. Carter briefly at one of those gatherings and it felt like I was in the company of a serene being.

In 1973, at the age of seventeen, I watched a young, Black and proud Angela Davis on television. She was giving a powerful speech, speaking out against a racist and corrupt police department run by J. Edgar Hoover and how they sought to end The Black Panther Party, falsely declaring them as a terrorist group. From that moment on, I vowed to be like Angela. I stopped having my long, coarse hair straightened. Imbued with the revolutionary theme song of James Brown, I cloaked myself with the mantra of "Say it loud, I'm Black and I'm proud."

I graduated from high school that summer proudly wearing my cap and gown and coarse afro. My mother must have wondered about me. She might even have been a bit disappointed because it was sort of her Saturday evening ritual to straighten my and my sister's hair for church on Sunday.

Mama had been our family's Rock of Gibraltar. Because of her, my siblings and I have built upon a life foundation consisting of morals, values, compassion and empathy for others. Mama left us the gift of "sowing seeds" to others.

As I turn the corner to my golden years, I feel the best I've ever felt, and am becoming the best I've ever been. I will continue to pour into the urgency for change and protest all the injustices that plague people of color in this country. The murder and abuse of innocent children, the gang wars, the gun violence, immigrant children housed in cages; the homelessness and unfair evictions in the housing arena, the killings of our Black men and women who are silenced by the hands of racist cops and the ways young Black boys and girls are portrayed in an often biased media.

My protests are in my writings which I view as weapons of awareness, as a POTUS racist White House agenda steeped in lies and distortions continues to rain destruction and division upon our democracy and freedoms. Such divisive agendas that attempt to silence our voices, keep us from standing up, speaking out and bringing awareness, must be dealt with.

I am encouraged by the rise and momentum of so many voices of America's youth that we are witnessing in the 21st century, who are strong and revolting against the status quo that seems hell bent on destroying America's freedoms. Although the sound of my voice dims in physical protests, it's my writing that speaks for the voiceless. It's where I protest the most. Although I lived through injustice, most of my childhood memories are of happier times.

The most poignant were when my siblings and I would gather in mama and daddy's bedroom to listen to their stories. Some stories entertained us, some scared us, and some would become life lessons for us to carry into adulthood. I suppose if I had stayed in Mississippi, my life would have been different, but I will always be that girl child who came into the world screaming and hollering and protesting.

BREATHING IN AMERICA

Annette M. Alston

Maybe it's a wintery mixture of DNA infused with life's frustrations and setbacks. Perhaps it's the questions that gnaw and chip at one's sense of being as you search for meaning. Yearning to sculpt with direction and purpose a masterpiece that forces the world to see and be seen more clearly. But it could just be my mom's fault.

Can't really blame Dad too much, because his temperament was very different from Mom's. He is a family man, Christian, was Superintendent of Sunday School and a deacon working two and three jobs for most of his life. He believed in non-violence and turning the other cheek. This didn't really disqualify him from being an activist. After all, no one can ever say Dr. King wasn't an activist. In fact, Dad was at the 1963 March on Washington, probably initially glad that Mom couldn't go 'cause she was pregnant with my brother Louis, while I was only a toddler.

No one knew how things would jump off at this event. I don't think anyone was expecting a picnic-like atmosphere. Mom had already made it known that she was not the non-violent type. So I think Dad might have been a little relieved that she was in no shape to take the train to DC. Dad's racial antennae didn't appear as fine-tuned as my mom's. Dad grew up with more privileges than Mom. He graduated from DeWitt Clinton High School in the Bronx. His mother was a social worker and public school teacher. His father was an insurance broker for businesses and a World War I vet. And clearly, they had decided to shelter their children as much as anyone could in post-WWII America. As racists paraded up Bailey Avenue, Grandpa kept him away from the window, where white-supremacist lights were flickering in the black night. One day, a white man grabbed their little son and he came home and told his mother. Grandma marched her son right up to that white man, gave him a history lesson and explained what would happen if he put his hands on her son ever again. Dad felt well-protected.

8

There was a comforting illusion of freedom, of security, in New York. My family was one of the first on the block to kick the icebox to the curb and haul in a Frigidaire. There were tons of Christmas presents under the tree for my father and uncle every year my grandfather was alive. It did become difficult after my grandfather passed. My father was 11 and my uncle was only six then. Black people couldn't get health insurance back then. So, when Grandpa broke some ribs after falling off of a ladder, much of the savings went toward paying hospital bills. One of the last things my grandfather did was go to South Carolina to sell the family home. He took his share to put aside for his sons' education. On the day he got off the train, he was taken straight to the Bronx VA Hospital. My father and uncle, waiting at home in expectation of seeing their Dad upon his return, would not see him again alive.

Race didn't hang over my father's family's lives, but it was there. Dad hung out with the white kids in his neighborhood during the week and the Black kids on the weekend from his church in Harlem. There were a few encounters he had with racism—his third-grade teacher scolding him for passing a note to a white girl, that time he had to beat up a white kid for calling him out of his name. As an adult, there were times he was assured over a phone conversation, of a position or in one case a space to open his camera store at a new mall, only to arrive to discover the job or space were no longer available. My Dad's Riverdale, Bronx accent did not match his Harlem River Drive hue in their eyes. Dad had seen enough to know that there had to be a change. But, he believed that change would come and believed in people to the point of recognizing the needs before seeing the faults. Dad's racism antennae would grow sharper with time. Yet, still appear dull compared to Mom's.

Mom's racial sense was sharp enough to rival a machete. She had a different incubation process. Her mom and dad were sharecroppers straight from Troy, Alabama. During the Great Migration, Grandma stole away with my six-year old uncle, four-year old mother and a set of infant twins on an evening train to Cairo, Illinois. Like many women of her generation, she did domestic work and picked crops to survive. They saved enough to buy a little house in Benton Harbor, Michigan. While there, Grandma managed to secure a job with Auto Specialists. Factory jobs paid well, but Grandma resented the fact that the factory bosses only gave her the jobs that men had, instead of the much-lighter work the white women were given. One day, Grandma's back couldn't take the load she was carrying any further and she slipped a disc. She had to be taken to the hospital for surgery, and, yes, she made sure she got Worker's Comp. My Mom was aware of all of this and made clear conclusions.

Mom had wanted to be a nurse ever since she was an 8-year-old child placed in a quarantine ward due to tuberculosis. She saw those nice nurses in starched white uniforms and pointed caps and she knew that's what she wanted to do with her life. She wanted to care for sick people the way the kind nurses had cared for her.

So, when her high school guidance counselor told her that she was not able to handle the courses that would put her on the path to becoming a registered nurse, but she might be able to become an LPN with the vocational classes she was placed in, something deep rose up in her. It may have been the first time she stood up to an adult. But you can't stand up for others until you can stand up for yourself. Mom took a deep breath and found her voice.

"I didn't say I wanted to be an LPN. I want to be an RN," my mother said.

"Well, Fannie, I don't think you can handle the college-bound classes."

My mother stood firm. "If I fail the classes then that is my problem."

The counselor put my mother in the classes my mom wanted, and she did struggle. But she eventually excelled and graduated. She went on to graduate from nursing school and passed the qualifying exam on the first go-round. I once asked her if she had ever gone back to that counselor. She said, "No. It was enough that I had succeeded where this woman thought I would fail."

These were among our family stories, our oral history heirlooms — the invisible parts of the family album. Stories that were infused in my DNA and became my baby's milk. One of my earliest memories was Mom dragging me along to a protest to keep a hospital open in New York. Then there was the time I thought my mother was going to jail on a very cold night just before Thanksgiving for demanding that the cab driver take us to Metropolitan Baptist Church. The white cab driver didn't want to go to Harlem. Mom told me not to budge out of my seat. She got out of the cab, made a call on the pay phone. I don't know who she spoke to, but the cab driver took us to Harlem and had to write a letter of apology to my mom. But it was in Newark, my home now, that I really learned about struggle from my parents.

After the Newark, NJ Rebellion of '67, some people thought it would be a good idea to hire some African American managers in S. Klein's Department Store downtown. Dad was promoted and moved from their New York Department store to the racially charged city of Newark. Economics dictated that the family follow. Only one problem, our first as incoming New Jerseyans: the apartment building that Mom was looking at was said to have no vacancies. Her antennae went up, as this was now familiar terrain. She knew her family's application would go into The Brown File, a.k.a. the circular file — like that time she was looking for a summer job in high school.

Mom decided to do what many Negroes-turned-Blacks did back then: she decided to test the rule, to see how brown the trash can was in that office. She reached out to her friend, Ursula, who was German. Mom went back to the apartment building office while Ursula waited down the hill. Mom was told once again that there were no vacancies. Mom met Ursula and then it was her turn. She went into the office carrying the same demographics, a husband and two children. Her white forms were signed, Ursula put down a deposit, and my parents inhaled and promptly took the office management to court. Black Power took all shades of resistance.

We moved to Newark three days after the assassination of Dr. King, right after parts of the city again went up in flames. After living there a short while, they realized that management was not keeping up the property as the apartment complex was getting rapidly less white. And not necessarily more Black. The Ivy Hill section of Newark was dubbed The Little UN because there were more than two-hundred languages represented from all over the world in this one enclave. I learned here that targets of racism were not limited to Black people. We stopped seeing maintenance workers picking up trash, among other issues. Mom and Dad started having tenant association meetings in their apartment. Mom had enlisted us to pass out the flyers under doors and behind doorknobs. We were in charge of 250 Mt. Vernon Place. The Rothmans took charge of 240 Mt. Vernon Place. There were fifteen floors in each of the buildings. Fortunately, everyone didn't come because there would not have been enough room.

It didn't stop at the tenant meetings. They would go to protests and regularly attend board meetings. I remember seeing Mom on a brand-new Black public-affairs show on WNBC-TV Channel 4, *Positively Black*. She stood and spoke, visibly angry with hair blowing and my two-year-old brother Jonathan in her arms. She was describing the mob scene in front of a school. White parents were actively trying to keep Black kids from being bussed to my elementary school.

Mom was the firebrand and Dad was the dove. But there were moments when the dove became more of a phoenix. There was the block association meeting that my parents started when we finally moved into a house on West End Avenue. The meeting was at our house. Mom had the flyers made up, and what was normal for our household by now, my brothers and I were tasked with distributing them up and down the block. I guess the meeting was getting somewhat heated because I remember one Italian American man said something about "you people." I was in another room half paying attention until I heard my father's voice question that man in a *Have-you-lost-your-mind and I'm-about-to-give-you-an-education* tone.

"What do you mean, 'you people'?"

Uh-oh. It was on. When Dad "The Dove" flipped, it generally startled people enough to create complete silence.

At that point, all this guy could do was stammer. "I didn't mean..."

The maxim goes that your first teachers are your parents. Mine taught me that when something needs to be done, you do it. If there is something that needs to be said, say it. I guess that's why on my very first day at Rutgers University on Livingston Campus, when my roommate and I were told about a Black Student Union Meeting, I knew I had to be there. We demanded that Rutgers divest from apartheid South Africa. Why shouldn't the athletic center be named after the extraordinary man, Paul Robeson? Mom and Dad half-expected they would have to get me out of jail one day. But they never said anything.

When I graduated from protests on campus, I was on the streets because the struggles didn't disappear. I had to march for those that no longer could and speak for those whose voices were silenced.

There was a 66-year-old grandmother, Eleanor Bumpurs, two shot gun blasts by NY cop, Stephen Sullivan. His charges were dropped. I felt pain but didn't hit the street again until it was on my back door. Too close to home. Philip Pannell was only 14 years old in 1990, shot in the back by Teaneck police officer Gary Spath. He was acquitted, while Pannell's family still grieves. That was it. I hit the pavement with others enraged, protesting against an ancient evil. If it visited my home, it could destroy me. I had to ameliorate it first. I have two younger brothers. It could have been them.

Abdul Louima, cops finally did some time. But not with Danette "Strawberry" Daniels, Amadou Diallo, Daniel Reyes, Rayshawn Brown, or Leroy Jermaine Grant. Earl Faison's torturers and murdering cops did get some time for civil rights violations, but not for murder. The marching and demonstrating hasn't stopped because the deaths and abuse never has. There was Stanton Crew, Sean Bell, Kashad Ashford, Abdul Kamal, and Jerame Reid. Fourteen-year -old Radazz Hearns survived, while 12-year-old Tamir Rice did not. Then there were Eric Garner, Michael Brown, Sandra Bland, Breonna Taylor, and George Floyd. Trayvon Martin and Ahmaud Arbery — killed by devils that thought they were cops who thought they could get away with it. Zimmerman did.

A trail of tears swells a river of rage.

Protesting against police brutality and for thorough and efficient education is my contribution to creating an America where we can all breathe.

My parents who love me, raised their voices and created my first breath. They know protest is in the air and I must inhale.

Now my folks follow this pattern: They just exhort me to be careful, ask me what meeting I am running off to next, and then they shake their heads, knowing there is nothing to be done but whisper a prayer to the sweet wind of the Holy Spirit.

READING INVISIBLE MAN

after Ralph Ellison

Marianne Taylor

one summer at Hoboken Paints
sixteen and giddy despite two busses
an eager receptionist disconnecting Joe
with his outta sight mustache and ponytail
telling him my father would never let me
date a factory man being one himself
and anyway I knew Joe's payday loans
paid for pot not grandma's meds

    and for Honors English I read that Optic White
    sold better than any color at the company
    so much need for whitewashing
    a world awash in white and hate and
    underneath the subway grate amid
    a million bulbs a bright mind burned unseen

my new friend Joseph came from Nigeria
by way of Trinity College and offered to share
his umbrella while we waited on Main
for bus No. 9 beside the limestone bank
he sounded British so polite and said
this summer job was lucrative but fumes
were deadly he was counting days and
people like Joe shouldn't see us together
beneath this white umbrella in the rain
so when we approached the factory Joseph
ran ahead, a shadow imperceptible in the fog

    and I read of the black college president
    and the white trustee, the false brothers,

the obliterated tenants and workers and the riots
and all those bulbs popped

and I asked Joseph

and he said no he would not share lunch
on the lawn of Hoboken Paints it was not time
to be seen it was only the seventies after all

A COLORIST IN RECOVERY

Stephanie J. Gates

My father was the color of coffee-black. My mother — coffee with lots of cream. And me — somewhere in between. Though I grew up with a solid sense of self, there were days when the cloud of colorism loomed over me and not only blocked the sun of my own beauty from shining, but also the beauty of Black people as a whole. I was a colorist and didn't know it.

I remember hearing people describe attractive people by their complexions — light. Their hair — "good" meaning not kinky. Their eyes pretty if they were any other color than dark brown. Their noses small and narrow and their lips thin. Their cheekbones — high. I remember how often people bragged of having Indian in their family or some other minuscule trace of another race. It was better to have had some "mixed" blood than to have been 100% Black. What else could account for the light-colored eyes or straight hair?

I remember when new babies were born and the family would look at the fingers and ears to determine the baby's coloring. I thought it was strange, but I never questioned why it was customary to check for complexion. I remember elders explaining to parents how to reduce the appearance of an "African" nose by gently stroking the sides of the nostrils in an effort to make the nose look less flat.

These memories I unconsciously carried with me and acted them out. I heard that light-skinned people looked better, and the images that I saw on TV and in magazines were of white women with bouncing and behaving hair. Though the women who graced the pages of *Ebony* and *Jet* were Black, they weren't brown like me. The message was clear: A European aesthetic was what we should aspire to, and in the absence of whiteness, lightness would do.

As a little girl, I loved to draw, and I loved to color. And my artwork reflected the overt and covert messages I received about beauty. I liked drawing women, I guess because I was a girl. So, I drew busty women with long hair. I colored their skin peach and their hair yellow. And that went on until the Black is Beautiful movement came into being and I had a come-to-Black-Jesus moment. I traded in the peach crayon for brown, and the yellow for black. I drew women and men with giant afros, clad in brightly colored dashikis wearing platform shoes. One day, I was drawing and my teacher, an older white woman, forbade me to draw people with afros anymore. I didn't question my teacher, but I didn't let it go either. I told my mother who sent my older sister to investigate. My teacher explained that I drew the afros too big. She folded one of my drawings in half to demonstrate that the afro was as big as the body. A "compromise" was reached in which I was allowed to draw people with afros as long as their hair didn't dwarf their bodies. This was one of the incidents that would shape my activism. It was my first lesson in self advocacy.

I was loving Blackness! For Easter, I begged my mother to allow me to wear a 'fro instead of the traditional press and curl. I loved that little girl with the big halo of hair. I have a picture of me from that day, and it is one of my favorites. The fascination with my natural hair was short-lived and I soon returned to the "real world" of straight hair: the press and curl.

The summer I graduated from eighth grade, I hung out with my older cousins and the cloud of colorism was hovering. My cousins had a friend who had a brother and he was beautiful to me. He had the wavy hair that I coveted, and if I couldn't have it myself, the boys I liked could. One day I saw him talking to a slue-footed, fair-skinned girl with long, wavy sandy-colored hair. I didn't think that she looked better than me, I just thought she had a better chance because she "was light skinned with 'good' hair." I found out later that she liked him, but he didn't like her. He liked me!

I was getting along fabulously until my sophomore year of high school when I learned that I had to take swimming every day for 10 weeks. It wasn't swimming that was the problem; it was my hair! I couldn't get my hair pressed every day and the alternative of "nappy" hair was out of the question. So, I asked my mother if I could get a relaxer. She reluctantly agreed and I was on the creamy crack for the next ten years.

At the same time that I started teaching, I was also undergoing a personal transformation. Thanks to an African American Women in Literature class in undergrad, I was reading stories about women who looked like me and faced the same issues I faced. There were patterns among the women's stories and one recurring pattern was a reckoning with some aspect of their appearance. The women were trying to be comfortable in their skin. And for many of them it meant giving up unrealistic beauty standards.

I was teaching African American students and we were reading "Revolt of the Evil Fairy," a short story in which the protagonist is a dark-skinned boy who wants to be Prince Charming in the annual school rendition of *Sleeping Beauty,* but there is an unwritten rule that the good characters must be played by light-skinned children and the bad characters by dark-skinned children. Well, he didn't care that he was dark and set out to win the role of Prince Charming because he had a huge crush on the fair-skinned, light-eyed, long, straight-haired girl cast as Sleeping Beauty. Before we could discuss the story, a dark-skinned girl in my class mumbled, "My color is a curse. I hate being so dark." I was taken aback. Surely this child coming of age during this period of multi-culturalism did not have the same issues that I grew up with? Yes, she did. And so did many of my students.

Though everyone tried to tell her that she was beautiful and that there was nothing wrong with her complexion, she was not convinced. She looked around the room and said, "I'm the darkest person in my family and the darkest person in this class. Nobody can tell me anything." And me, with my caramel coloring knew that she was not listening to anything I had to say, and so I set out to show her that dark girls and women are beautiful, too.

There was not a great deal of material available initially, but over time I began to find some articles and books that could help me explain this phenomenon to my students. We watched movies and documentaries that tackled the topic. The process was life-changing because for me to help my students, I had to recognize by own biases, and check my colorist thinking. *How was I judging myself? How was I judging others? Did I hold people to a narrowly defined concept of beauty based on European standards?* Though, people on either end of the color spectrum seem to be the most affected by colorism, being in the middle of the color spectrum doesn't let me off the hook. It's a complex and nuanced issue that's not limited to skin color.

Colorism is also about the intersection of hair length and texture, facial features and body image. When I was growing up, big booties were a rarity outside of our community. And many of us were ridiculed for our backsides. We were not praised like we are today. All of these aspects of appearance play a role in how we are perceived as well as how we perceive others.

For me, hair was the biggest hurdle. It took years for me to make peace in my head with what was on my head. I wear my hair short and natural. I love the freedom my hair gives me. Other women have had to come to terms with the way they came into the world. It is my goal to make it easier for the girls—and the boys coming up now. I want the sun to shine brightly on their beauty from a clear blue sky.

Learning that colorism was alive and thriving, I decided to write my thesis on intra-racial prejudice, which is the term I used at the time. I wanted to see what the data revealed about light-skinned/dark-skinned, good hair/bad hair etc. in the lives of my students. It was showing up in my classes regularly. I had some girls threaten to cut another girl's face and hair because she was light-skinned with long, loosely curled hair. The girls who wanted to fight her were jealous. I had dark-skinned girls who hated being dark. I had light-skinned boys who were loved by the girls but bullied by the boys for not being "Black enough" or "man enough" because "real" Black men and boys are dark. I had little girls with heads weighed down with weave, and girls whose hair had been eaten away by chemicals that were too strong. I had students choosing playmates by skin tone. I had brown and dark-skinned boys who tried to convince me that light-skinned girls look better. The stories kept coming year after year, and the stories keep coming now as I'm in my 28th year of teaching.

It breaks my heart to see students still dealing with the same issues associated with colorism. To hear a dark-skinned girl explain to me that she would have been born light-skinned if she had not been premature. In addition to writing my thesis on intra-racial prejudice, I have made the awareness of and eventual eradication of colorism my life's work.

Every year, I teach on the topic of colorism. Early in my teaching career, I used to temporarily separate my students by skin color and watch as they took on and accused each of stereotypical behaviors associated with skin tone — dark-skinned girls are mean; light-skinned girls are stuck up.

We talk about the color caste system in our communities. My students are now African American and Latino and I show them how both groups have colorist behaviors. I challenged my Latino students to watch telenovelas and report back what they notice about the casting. I had students bring in pictures of women they thought were attractive to show them that they too were colorists. Most of the pictures that they brought in were of light-skinned or white celebrities. I have been both teacher and learner in this process. One time, I was talking to a group of girls about colorism, and they encouraged me to watch music videos. They explained that if it was a booty-shaking song, the girls were dark and if it was a love song, the love interest was always light.

A few years ago, I teamed up with a Mexican teacher at my school and together we did a workshop for the staff on how colorism shows up in both the Latinx and the African American communities. It is a problem in communities of color around the world.

I have taken what I've learned and created workshops on colorism. I've done it at the local and national levels for anyone who wants to learn about the impact of colorism in our lives. To combat colorism, I created the *Pretty is Me/Handsome I Am Project* which is an annual event to celebrate the diversity of beauty in my school. I recruited a committee of staff members to work with me, and together we created lesson plans and activities that showcase how pretty and handsome students are. We've constructed runways for the students to strut their stuff. Two years ago, I won the ActUp Award which was a $1,000.00 grant for my *Pretty is Me/Handsome I Am Project*. That year, I was able to take photos, create collages of their faces and mount the collages on the wall on the first floor for everyone to see. I was also able to hire a motivational speaker to talk to the students about self-esteem.

My dream is to take my show on the road and travel the world educating people about colorism, which is a subset of racism. It is a serious problem that needs to be addressed. Colorism can factor into schooling, policing, sentencing, employment, marriage, housing, and many other things that impact quality of life. I recognize how colorism clouded my life in my youth, and I'm ready to share what I've learned with others. I am a colorist in recovery, and I'm on a mission to rescue others.

THE CONFINEMENT CAGE

Erin Goseer Mitchell

My hometown, Fitzgerald, GA is located in south/central Georgia, two-hundred miles south of Atlanta. Several years after the public schools were integrated, a former resident and graduate of our "colored school," Monitor, suggested that a tradition of a tri-annual Grand Homecoming be put in place. Later, Queensland, the former "colored" school in the county, was included.

Over the years, I returned for many Grand Homecoming festivities. When I returned in 2013, I drove by the north side of the Ben Hill County Courthouse. I quickly glanced at something on the lawn I'd never seen before. Curiosity got the best of me and I went back the next day to take a closer look. What I saw shocked and hurt beyond belief. This horse-drawn, lattice-work iron cage was about the size of a small train caboose. I took a picture of the inscription. This is what it said:

> This historical portable containment cage was purchased by Ben Hill County from Manley Steel in the year 1913 for the purpose of transporting and housing the chain gang convicts while working on county roads.

When I read this and looked at more details of the cage, I felt ill. There was a ramp on the back end. I imagined men walking up this ramp with large iron balls attached by a chain to their ankles, thus the name of "chain gang." Ceiling to floor vertical poles, similar to ones on city subways, were on both sides of the cage. Short benches were on both sides at the front end. I imagined these were seats for the guards who carried rifles. As a child, I had seen men in bold black and white striped suits and caps working on street infrastructure building projects. I had seen the guards/overseers on the streets as the men worked.

I could not get this horrible image out of my head. Since I'd never seen this confinement cage before, I wondered where it had been all of the years after it was no longer used. I wondered why it was brought to the Courthouse grounds. When I continued to feel consumed by thought of this wagon, I wrote a letter to seven prominent citizens/leaders in Fitzgerald. I kept a copy of my original letter to the leaders for many years. I discarded it when I could let go of the painful memories it stirred. I remember asking such questions as:

Where was it stored when it was no longer used?

When was it placed on the Courthouse grounds?

Why was it placed there?

What was its meaning and purpose for these times and this location?

Would it serve a meaningful purpose as a teaching tool if it were placed on the Museum grounds?

Three of the seven people I contacted responded. One person's response was that this was a part of our culture and heritage and should be preserved. I did not send a letter to the curator of the Blue and Gray Museum, but her response was, "Never! I don't want that evil relic on our Museum grounds."

Another man, a local politician and influencer responded that he agreed with me that it should not be on the Courthouse grounds, but he would need the support and cooperation of his colleagues to have it removed. Tim Anderson, editor of the local newspaper, *The Fitzgerald-Herald Leader,* and Sherri Butler, features page editor, also responded. Sherri responded via email that my letter was passionate, eloquent, well-written, and absolutely right. She said that she did not want to see it at the museum either. Tim wrote in an editorial that he had received a letter from a former resident expressing concerns about the appropriateness of the confinement cage on the courthouse grounds. He said that Fitzgerald was better than this, that there were too many good things and great people in Fitzgerald to have this negative relic in such a prominent place. At first, Tim didn't disclose my name, only saying a former resident had posed these questions. As time went on and the discussions became more heated, he gave my full name, Erin Goseer Mitchell, as the person who had first asked questions about the confinement cage.

I don't know what took place in the town, politically or otherwise, to have the cage removed. One year later, in November 2015, Tim, in an email, told me that the cage was being removed that day. In the next edition of the newspaper, there was a picture of a large flat-bed truck with the wagon on it. The caption under the picture was brief, just stating that it was being removed. Tim didn't write an editorial about it.

When I returned to Fitzgerald seven months later, I saw that the wagon was removed and the lawn restored. I felt relieved that I had done a little bit to make sure that this valiant and inhumane history of how Black people were treated was no longer positioned as something to feature and celebrate.

Scene from

ANY OTHER NAME

Brian C. Billings

(Lights rise to half intensity on the grounds of Earlian Middle School in April. The lunch period has just begun. A patch of worn and faded brick is painfully visible SL of the school's front doors. An engraved plaque featuring one of Dennis Earlian's more famous poems once rested in this spot; recent activism has led to its removal. A metal chain-link fence completely encircles the statue of Earlian. A sign on the fence warns that the enclosure is electrified. A yellow wash rises CS on the interior of PRINCIPAL FREDERICK BALL's office. Facing DS, HE sits behind his desk in an impressive leather chair. His desk is bare save for a stack of files, a computer, and a cup of pens behind the monitor. SADIE BRIGHTWATER, HECTOR MARTINEZ, and KASHYRA MILLS sit in hard plastic chairs in front of the desk. HECTOR is hiding slightly behind KASHYRA. Their seats are angled out.)

FREDERICK BALL

I'm sorry to pull you out of lunch, but this is the only time I could have all three of you together.

SADIE BRIGHTWATER

I've been asking for an appointment since —

FREDERICK BALL

The PTA meeting. Yes. I'm aware. Please don't think I've been ignoring you, Miss Brightwater. Honestly, during your time here, ignoring you has *never* been a possibility.
(HE opens one of the files and flips through it.)

Staging a formal protest against required PE classes. Hosting an after-school gathering to discuss how to start a recycling program. Demanding that student government have more say in blocking off

24

class times. Oh, and my favorite: a request to see the school budget. You were worried about funding inequality.

HECTOR MARTINEZ

I remember that. Football and soccer were getting like a quarter of the budget. That's unreal for a middle school.

FREDERICK BALL

So, we all found out. The newspaper ran a beautiful article. With color pictures, no less. I have more I could share, of course, but, somehow, it inevitably comes down to you three every time. Every. Single. Time.

KASHYRA MILLS

So, you're cheesed off. I get it.

FREDERICK BALL

You misunderstand me, Miss Mills. I like to think I've weathered all your little escapades with impressive forbearance.

HECTOR MARTINEZ

Grace under fire?

FREDERICK BALL

Thank you, Mister Martinez. That's exactly what I meant. I don't run this school like an ogre patrolling a castle. I believe in listening to the students. I ask teachers for their input. It's a practical lesson in democracy.

SADIE BRIGHTWATER

It's not a democracy, though.

KASHYRA MILLS

Hector says the whole country's not even a democracy.

FREDERICK BALL

A lesson, I said.

HECTOR MARTINEZ
But democracy means simple majority rules. Everyone has a vote. That's *not* what we've got. I did a report on that. They've got these schools in Massachusetts called Sudbury schools —

FREDERICK BALL
A republic, then.

HECTOR MARTINEZ
That's not really right, either.

FREDERICK BALL
Fine! It's a benevolent dictatorship! Let's just say that I do the best I can.

SADIE BRIGHTWATER
I know, Mister Ball. You could've come down hard on us lots of times, but you didn't. You're a pretty good guy.

FREDERICK BALL
I'm glad to hear you say that.

KASHYRA MILLS
What she said.

HECTOR MARTINEZ
Don't push it, Shyra.

SADIE BRIGHTWATER
This is about taking down the statue, isn't it?

FREDERICK BALL
You've put me in a bad situation, Miss Brightwater.

KASHYRA MILLS
Bad? I'll tell you what's bad. Dennis Earlian. He was a bad man. He fought on the wrong side of a mean war for wrong reasons. He wanted to keep his slaves, and when he couldn't do that, he wanted to keep 'em from bein' treated like people.

FREDERICK BALL

I can't say you're entirely wrong, Miss Mills. You see, I know my history, too, and I understand your concerns about Dennis Earlian. People have brought up the matter before. How could we avoid it? Eighty percent of our students are African American.

HECTOR MARTINEZ

Eighty-four percent.

FREDERICK BALL

Yes. Eighty-four percent. Let's be current. But that PTA meeting didn't limit itself to taking down a statue honoring a flawed man.

SADIE BRIGHTWATER

A racist.

FREDERICK BALL

A deeply, *horribly* flawed man. Okay? Good. The issue that got handed to me when I came back from my conference, however, was changing the name of the whole school. And that's a much bigger problem.

KASHYRA MILLS

I'll bet it's the Earlians. They called down and told you to shut us up.

FREDERICK BALL

The Earlians haven't had any direct involvement with the school in over sixty years. We've been on state funding for a good long while. It's not them I'm worried about. It's tradition. *Earlian* is the name of this school. It's where we vote and have the bicycle rodeo. That name's ingrained across generations.

KASHYRA MILLS

Yeah, yeah. We've heard the speech.

FREDERICK BALL

Well, this time you'd better listen. For most people in this city, the name Dennis Earlian . . . it's like background noise. You hear it all the time. I guarantee your average guy or gal doesn't know doodly-squat about the man other than the basics. You say he was a nasty piece of work.

That's personal history. What people really care about is *community* history. They have a stake in the Earlian name that stands for this school, where we've graduated good and solid citizens — including me and your mother, Miss Mills. We've been a center for education and a sign for progress; we give people back to their families a little more concerned for the world and a bit smarter than they were when they came through our doors. When people hear our name, the first thing they think of is the good we've done, not the sins of one misguided man.

SADIE BRIGHTWATER
Misguided. Flawed. You have a hard time blaming him. I know you like his poetry.

FREDERICK BALL
I like the *style* of his poetry ... but poetry's more than politics. And it wasn't so long ago that I was sitting where you are dreaming about being a writer — a poet — and needing an example to follow. I wanted to find somebody in this place who felt the same wonder for words that I did. Can you blame me for reaching out to a poet with a statue attached? You don't find many of those in a small town, Miss Brightwater. I didn't care about what he'd done; I only cared about the fact that I thought I could probably write like him.

HECTOR MARTINEZ
You never read your poetry to us.

FREDERICK BALL
That's because I stink. I'm a much better principal. My point is that it was the idea of Dennis Earlian — the noble poet — that inspired me and not the actual person. This school's name does the same thing for its students ... or at least it tries. Call me idealistic, but I can't stand by and watch that name and its heritage get erased by a moment of fashionable propaganda.

SADIE BRIGHTWATER
Other schools don't think it's propaganda.

HECTOR MARTINEZ
I've got a list if you want it.

FREDERICK BALL
It doesn't matter, Mister Martinez. Other schools aren't this school.
We have our own environment with unique concerns, and I have to
act in the best interest of those concerns.

KASHYRA MILLS
You're not gonna sponsor us, huh? You're not gonna let us talk to
the Board?

FREDERICK BALL
I'm sorry. No.

SADIE BRIGHTWATER
Haven't you gotten any letters? We have a lot of people who said
they'd write.

FREDERICK BALL
Oh, I've been really popular lately. Letters. E-mails. Facebook posts.
You name it. I know you think that all these people are on your
side . . . but they're not. I've gotten just as many folks against you
as for you. I support your initiative, and I know we can do
something about the statue. Frankly, all your buzz about it makes
the thing almost irresistible to a certain type. I've had the janitors
scrubbing off graffiti all last month, so, yes, let's take care of that
problem. Anything past the statue . . . there's not much I can do. I'm
confident you'll have the same answer from the Board if you
manage to get there.

HECTOR MARTINEZ
Show him, Shyra.

KASHYRA MILLS
Sadie?

SADIE BRIGHTWATER
Yeah. Show him.

(KASHYRA hands a card to PRINCIPAL BALL. HE takes it with a touch of caution.)

FREDERICK BALL
What's this?

KASHYRA MILLS
Our website.

FREDERICK BALL
You mean your petition. I've seen it. I asked you to put a hold on that, remember?

(HE tries to hand back the card.)

HECTOR MARTINEZ
You haven't seen the page today. *Míralo*. Please.

SADIE BRIGHTWATER
Look it up on your computer.

(PRINCIPAL BALL turns to his computer as SHE talks. HE brings up his browser and types in the address from the card. HE takes a beat when the page comes up.)

Whose picture is that?

FREDERICK BALL
Mine.

KASHYRA MILLS
Notice the caption. Thirty-six-point font.

SADIE BRIGHTWATER
It flashes, too.

KASHYRA MILLS
Wicked, huh?

FREDERICK BALL
"Our Principal, Our Hero."

HECTOR MARTINEZ
Why don't you read the note?

FREDERICK BALL
"We're glad we're at a school where we can say how we feel. We're proud to have a principal who gives us a chance to make a difference. Thank you, Mister Ball." And these names . . . ?

SADIE BRIGHTWATER
I took a voting box around lunch yesterday. Those kids all go here. Most of them have parents who signed our petition. Some of the kids really wanted to make suggestions for a new name, so I told them to write their ideas on the voting slips.

KASHYRA MILLS
I sent a copy of the link to the superintendent.

HECTOR MARTINEZ
And Representative DeFornay.

SADIE BRIGHTWATER
And Shyra's mother.

KASHYRA MILLS
Not that she didn't know already. 'Course now she can send it all over the place. You know how much she loves to spread the news, don't you, Mister Ball? What can I say but "Got—!"

(SADIE has been watching PRINCIPAL BALL's face during KASHYRA's tirade. SHE gestures for SHYRA to stop.)

SADIE BRIGHTWATER
Shyra!

KASHYRA MILLS
Too much?

HECTOR MARTINEZ
Too much.

KASHYRA MILLS
Okay.

SADIE BRIGHTWATER
We just want to finish this, Mister Ball. Like you said, it's up to the Board in the end. I do understand how you feel, though. You know I do. And I think you want us to go on. Why else would you talk to us like this when you could have just called our parents?

HECTOR MARTINEZ
It's like a civics lesson.

KASHYRA MILLS
Nice one, Hector.

(A beat passes as PRINCIPAL BALL contemplates.)

FREDERICK BALL
I assume you brought something for me to sign. The sponsorship?

SADIE BRIGHTWATER
Yes, sir.

(SHE hands him a form that SHE has been hiding in her lap. HE casts about for a pen. HECTOR takes one out of the mug on the desk and hands it over. PRINCIPAL BALL signs. KASHYRA rips the paper out of his hands.)

KASHYRA MILLS
I'll take that. Thanks bunches.

HECTOR MARTINEZ
Muchas gracias.

SADIE BRIGHTWATER
Yes.

FREDERICK BALL
Lunch is nearly over. You'd better hurry if you want to eat anything.

KASHYRA MILLS
C'mon, Hector. Let's hit it.

(THEY exit. SADIE moves to follow them, but SHE turns to PRINCIPAL BALL.)

FREDERICK BALL
Go on, Miss Brightwater. They'll leave you behind.

(SHE crosses to him and holds out a palm. HE takes it as if to shake it, but SHE covers his hand with her other hand and pulls so that HE is forced to look into her eyes.)

SADIE BRIGHTWATER
Thank you.

(SHE releases his hand abruptly. HE falls back lightly and ends up sitting on his desk while holding out his hand. SHE exits. Blackout.)

SOCIAL JUSTICE

I GAVE PEACE A CHANCE

Terri Elders

"My Great Uncle Loring once shook hands with Abraham Lincoln," my grandmother used to brag, her eyes twinkling, her entire face wreathed with pride. "This was right after the Emancipation Proclamation. And everybody in our family has voted Republican since."

I never suspected I'd be the first in the family to stray from that faithful fold. But at 2:00 a.m. on October 14, 1960, Senator John F. Kennedy addressed a crowd of shivering students on the steps of the Union at the University of Michigan. In his speech, delivered just weeks before the national elections, he'd challenged these students to devote two years of their lives to helping people in developing countries.

When I heard Kennedy's ringing words on the radio later that morning, I tried to picture myself boarding a plane and heading for Tanganyika where I would teach toddlers to read. Though married and a young mother, I envied those students who might have this chance to serve.

But it was never going to happen, I told myself. First, it was unlikely Kennedy could get elected. Nobody in my family or my husband's thought that the young man from Massachusetts could divert enough votes from frontrunner Nixon. I, myself, had registered as a Republican when I'd turned twenty-one.

Second, I was married, had a toddler, and was working toward a degree to become an English teacher. When I mentioned Kennedy's proposal to my husband, he just laughed. "There's children right here in Los Angeles County who need to learn to read. You don't have to go overseas to make your dreams come true," he pointed out.

When I went to the voting booth on Election Day, I hesitated. Until that very day, I hadn't made up my mind. But as I entered my booth, I steeled myself and decided. Even if I couldn't have that chance to serve, I'd still advocate for those who could. So, I voted for Kennedy, knowing that my husband would tease me later about our votes canceling each other.

A few months later, I privately thrilled to JFK's inaugural address. I had always scoffed at the notion that I belonged to a so-called Silent Generation, an uninspiring label for those young adults of the Eisenhower years. Now Kennedy insisted that the torch be passed to a new generation of Americans, one that could be vocal and active. I vowed to be part of that generation.

My husband had been right, of course, about people needing help at home as well as overseas. I continued with my studies, eventually getting a teaching credential and settling into becoming a high school English and journalism teacher right where we lived, in Long Beach.

The day of Kennedy's assassination, I sent my stunned students repeatedly to the nurse's office for more boxes of Kleenex. I turned on the classroom radio and we listened together as the horrific story unfolded. I thought about Great- Great-Great-Uncle Loring, and wished I'd had the opportunity to shake Kennedy's hand. Now it would never be.

A few years later, after riots rocked our inner cities, I abandoned teaching to become a caseworker to help rebuild South Central Los Angeles. My parents had a tough time understanding this. They remembered the Depression years and chose to think I was working in a soup kitchen. No matter how much I tried to explain about Lyndon Johnson's War on Poverty and the Equal Opportunity Act, they insisted upon telling friends, "Terri's working for The Dole." I suspect they imagined me wrapped in a big white apron, ladling out soup. Eventually I returned to graduate school and earned an MSW (Master of Social Welfare) at UCLA.

I survived the turbulent sixties and seventies, the long war in Vietnam. Reading the body counts on the front page of my *Los Angeles Times*, I'd pause and reflect on the Beatles anthem, "Give Peace a Chance."

Then finally, at fifty, divorced, my son grown, I remembered something I'd read that the first Peace Corps director, Sargent Shriver had once said: "There is an alternative to war. It has been with us forever."

At long last, in 1987 I ran away from home and joined the Peace

Corps. Friends raised both eyebrows and issues: "Aren't you a bit, how shall I put this, uhhhh, *old*?" "Do you think you're up for mosquitoes and pit latrines?" "You know, don't you, that older people have a lot of trouble learning new languages?"

I developed some pat rejoinders. The Peace Corps recruiter told me that many seniors join. I would most likely end up living in towns or cities, not in the jungle in a mud hut. I could relearn my high school Spanish and college French, if need be.

I joined, rejoined, and then extended. As a Peace Corps Volunteer, I hacked open coconuts with a machete outside my house in Belize City. I clung to my counterpart as we raced on her motorcycle to get across streams before they flooded in the province of San Juan de la Maguana, Dominican Republic. I helped paint murals on the Youth Center fence with teens on a rare dry afternoon when the monsoon winds had died down in Mont Fleuri, Seychelles.

I gained more than I gave. I learned to appreciate living with less. I found fulfillment in working with people from every walk of life, from government officials to village entrepreneurs.

After a decade overseas, I returned to the States and became a health programming and training specialist at Peace Corps headquarters in Washington DC. In this capacity, I helped strengthen efforts of volunteers in dozens of countries to address malnutrition, HIV/AIDS, and the infectious diseases that lead to high infant mortality rates. I listened to gray wolves howling on the steppes outside Ulan Bator on the spring equinox in Mongolia. I thrilled to the spontaneous chorusing of a hymn by Samoan chiefs and missionaries at a suicide prevention training session in Apia, Samoa's capital. I explored the corners of the earth: Guyana, Uzbekistan, Thailand, St. Vincent, Bulgaria. What a world indeed the Peace Corps opened for me.

On January 29, 2002, Sargent Shriver, the brother-in-law of JFK, and founding director of the Peace Corps, appeared at the Directors Forum at Peace Corps Headquarters to address a packed audience of about two-hundred staffers. Frail, in the early stages of Alzheimer's, Shriver nonetheless read in a strong voice from his notes and emphasized that peace is more than just the absence of war. He described peace as "living together based on what we have in common. Our differences matter less than our kinship." I took notes.

After he spoke, he shook hands with dozens of us, nodding as we told him where we had served as volunteers.

"I'm honored to shake your hand," I told him. "I owe my whole life to you and to President Kennedy."

"I'm honored to shake yours," he said, squeezing my hand between his.

In subsequent years I've had several conversations with friends who've expressed interest in serving overseas. They range in age from early twenties to mid-sixties. I continue to participate in local recruitment events. So here I am today, still advocating for the Peace Corps...all because of a campaign speech by JFK over fifty years ago.

Surely by now Grandma would forgive me my 1960 vote. She, like Shriver, could recognize kinship. Sometimes when I'm feeling nostalgic for my childhood, I cheer myself by picturing her in heaven, shaking hands with Abraham Lincoln...and John F. Kennedy. Her eyes are still twinkling.

QUIET ACTIVIST

Susan M. Winstead

As I drove up the steep incline toward the gates of the United States Military Academy at West Point in upstate New York, the dialogue flowing from the radio was one of the first indicators something had changed in America — and not for the better.

I had just returned to the United States after serving four and a half years of military service in the Army overseas in Germany. During that time, the world had seen great change due to the Soviet Union falling as the Berlin Wall in Germany had been overwhelmed by citizens living east of the divided city. The overtaking of the wall had been the unintended consequence of a politician in East Berlin who misspoke about allowing passage to the other side. After nearly thirty years of repression, millions of people overtook the wall, when previously they would have been shot by the soldiers of the East German Army who guarded it.

The mission to deter war and maintain peace in the West caused the women and men who served in the U.S. military, and were stationed in West Germany, to experience a downsizing or what became known as 'the drawdown' in military circles. Though the unexpected Persian Gulf War created a brief reprieve, soldiers by the thousands who had hoped to 'put in their twenty and retire' were forced to leave the military and step into an unsympathetic civilian society.

So, hearing the words of the man criticizing the presence of women among the ranks of cadets at West Point came as a shock. Primarily because during my previous stateside tour of duty, before going to Germany, no one on the radio paid attention to the military. Radio stations seemed to be more about music and news, weather, and sports. But, as the weeks progressed into the months at my new stateside duty assignment on an Army sub-post outside of West Point, the dialogue from that particular person on that particular radio station criticized women in the military even though he had never served. He also disparaged public school teachers, college and university academics, private and public unions – everything that had stemmed from the Nazi regime – and resulted in the United States putting and maintaining a military presence in Germany. Still, he had an appeal and seemed to make himself relatable to the average working person.

Within the year of returning to the United States, I relocated from the northeast of the country to the southeast – glad to get away from the radio show broadcasting out of New York City. But, in my new community, not only did the radio station broadcast that program, but a local show with the same ideology followed. These radio talk show hosts glorified the military and raised alarming questions. I did not understand why they aligned themselves with the military, especially since they had never served in the Armed Forces. I wondered what they expected the military to do for them. My activism began when I would hear the most disparaging of comments made about women who served their country in the military. I would respond by mailing respectful letters to the host reminding him women served in jobs opened up to them when the military draft ended in the early 1970s.

After several years, I moved to the Midwest where I had grown up, only to find the radio station I had listened to with all of the latest rock & roll hits had become a talk radio station carrying the nationally syndicated show I had first heard when stationed in New York. Though the radio shows seemed more professional and less extreme, there were some exceptions. I again would respond by sending an email or mail a letter to explain why the information they broadcast was inaccurate.

One day though, I heard an interview conducted by two hosts – one male, one female. Neither of them had ever served in the military, and the interviewee was misleading them. The premise of the show centered on a recently released "Report from West Point" criticizing foreign policy and the sitting U.S. President Barack Obama.

I was skeptical about the existence of the "Report from West Point" since Army regulations and the Uniform Code of Military Justice prohibit military personnel from using 'contemptuous words' against a president, vice president, or Secretary of Defense. Showing political partisanship is also prohibited.

My inquiry to the radio show producer received a response from a program director who said they didn't understand the context of my concern and asked me to provide more detail. I sent another email, but never heard back from them.

I then wrote the Superintendent at West Point and asked him when it became practice for a service academy to release a report criticizing foreign policy and a sitting U.S. President. I understood that to be against protocol. Apparently, he obtained a transcript and listened to the show. I received a response and confirmed no 'report from West Point' existed. As a result of this situation, verifying information and journalistic ethics were brought to light in the radio community, plus, college and university journalism departments.

It was never my goal to spend my time writing letters to media outlets in order to question or challenge misinformation. In fact, I try my best to get a reprieve and simply enjoy listening to the radio. However, as these radio stations that previously played music become agents of damaging information, I simply cannot help but do what I can to insist the truth be told.

#StandOnEveryCorner

Rita Moe

It's 4:30 — rush hour —
and we're on the corner:
two septuagenarians named Rita
and a Corgi named Harvey.

We're halfway between her house and mine
on this little corner in the suburbs
where St. Anthony Village meets Roseville.

It's a five-corner stop and every car, truck,
school bus, motorcycle, and delivery van
on all five arms of this star
has to stop and look:
> At us,
> And at our signs.

Some signs are mounted on sawhorses:
> *Make America Kind Again*
> *Science Matters - Protect Our Planet*
Some lean against poles:
> *Reunite the Families*
> *Stop Corruption, Collusion, Criminality*
Rita Mix clamps one to her scooter basket:
> *Protect Social Security*
I hold cardboard over my chest like a shield:
> G.O.P. letters trapped behind prison bars

And we wave.
We wave the queenly wave —
> a metronome set on andante.

We wave the toddler wave—
    fingers flapping open and shut.
We wave the Here-I-Am-in-a-Crowd wave—
    broad overhead sweeps of the arm.
We wave the I-Can-Almost-Reach-You wave—
    arm outstretched and fingers rippling a keyboard.
What do drivers do?
They wave back.
They wave and smile.
They wave out of reflex.
They wave with thumbs up.
They wave and mouth *Thank you.*
They lift the tip of one finger from the steering wheel
    and give a slight nod.
They beep and blast and blare their horns.

There are detractors:
The frowners, head shakers, thumbs-downers,
finger flashers, tire squealers.
And yellers:
    MAGA
    Fake News
    Trump 2020
    Fucking idiots- Zero IQ

We look for the regulars:
The young woman in the pink VW.
The UPS truck driver that honks and waves
    every day at 4:50.
The Jimmy John's delivery kid with the big grin.
The commuting biker in the yellow helmet.
The woman in the hijab
    with three waving kids in the back seat.

It's October now.
We've been at this since August 13th.
When she can—weekends and days off—
Deb from Coon Rapids joins us
and a few enlistees make special appearances.

Mostly it's the two Ritas—Mix & Moe—
and, of course, Harvey,
    who sleeps, eats locust tree pods,
    scratches in the dirt,
    and barks *I'm the boss* at every passing dog.

At first it was audacious, a jump into mid-air.
We can't do this, can we?... Let's do it anyway.
A day or two on our own and soon
there'll be a crowd of protestors with us.

Well, no crowds so far.
But we're still here every day—4:30 to 5:30.
Maybe it's our version of an apple a day,
afternoon tea, or T'ai Chi.
Maybe it's a trick of endorphins,
triggered by the grins that sprout unbidden
on our faces at the first wacky wave of the day.

And we'll be here through Election Day.
Two Ritas, some signs, and a dog.
Here we stand.

#StandOnEveryCorner is a national movement started by Bryce Tache of Minneapolis on 6/20/2016 when he began a daily protest in his neighborhood. Read about it at www.southwestjournal.com and www.StandOnEveryCorner.

GAVAGE

Richard Downing

The North American hummingbird averages 75 wing beats per *second*
in normal flight.

This is *normal*? Or *this*?

According to *The New York Times,* the richest 1 percent now own more wealth
than the bottom 90 percent.

I'm going to check my portfolio — right after I look up
"portfolio."

I want
to know if I'm among the 1 percent.

I want
to know if the 1 percent drive 16-year-old Chevy Impalas
or if they drive cars with more exotic spellings like *Maserati* and *Porsche*
or if they have to drive at all.

I want
to know when to hold my bucket up
to catch the trickle down.

I want
to know if the 1 percent eat pasta, a lot of pasta.
I hope so. I eat a lot of pasta.

I want
to know if the 1 percent prefer *foie gras*? I looked that up too.
It means "fat liver." It does. My aunt had one, *had* one —
her prescription was out of reach.

I want
to know if my aunt failed
to hold her bucket up at the right time, the right place.

I want
to know if the rich buy guns or if just their "people" buy guns
and, if so, do their "people" sometimes hold those guns
the way I'd hold my bucket if I had a stronger grip.

I want
to know if the EPA can afford the psycho-
analysis necessary to uncover the source of its self-loathing.
It's probably the father. It's usually the father.
The first lady seems nice enough.

I want
to know how much food is in the President's Cabinet
and if there are expiration dates.

I want
to know why they work so hard to stamp
out Food Stamps.

I want
to know when hummingbird became a delicacy.

Note: The ruby-throated hummingbird (Archilochus colubris) migrates
from the Yucatan Peninsula across the Gulf of Mexico to Florida. This non-
stop flight burns more calories than an adult hummingbird normally
weighs; however, hummingbirds can double their fat mass in preparation
for their migration.

BEYOND CASSEROLES

Judy Seldin-Cohen

I bring my first foil-wrapped casserole for the homeless to my synagogue a year or two after I move to Charlotte. On cold winter nights, a local agency arranges to shelter people experiencing homelessness in multi-purpose rooms and fellowship halls. When it's my synagogue's turn to unfold twelve cots in a clean, safe, heated space, my supper club of newcomers to our congregation signs up to help.

Instead of meeting in one of our homes, a dozen of us bring an expanded version of our monthly potluck to the synagogue social hall. I make turkey tetrazzini—soft food that's not too spicy, accommodating teeth and bellies that might appreciate some gentleness. Despite the stark differences in where each of us will sleep that night, the supper club hosts find common ground with the synagogue's overnight guests as we all share a meal together.

The following winter, I bring a casserole to my friend Merle's townhouse. Every Christmas, our synagogue provides food for a homeless shelter to relieve the church volunteers immersed in their own holiday preparations. Merle organizes the synagogue collection, filling the refrigerators in both her kitchen and her garage with donations. Turkey tetrazzini in a foil casserole pan to feed the homeless again.

My volunteer work for those experiencing homelessness expands beyond casseroles. I scrub a bathtub in an abandoned apartment building, soon to be repurposed as temporary housing for homeless families. I participate in creating an affordable housing documentary, dispelling the Not-In-My-Back-Yard myths that circulate in prosperous neighborhoods. I spearhead a user-friendly website, guiding volunteers to agencies in the homelessness services network. I troubleshoot for a multi-agency pilot program, resulting in a community-wide furniture ministry. I join an interfaith group of congregation volunteers, spawning a rental subsidy program.

Much of this housing and homelessness work evolves in collaboration with my synagogue rabbi, coincidentally also named Judy. Rabbi Judy's voice in the community creates a new dynamic for me. Southerners often ask new acquaintances, "Where do you go to church?" Responding that I go to synagogue led to awkward pauses when I lived elsewhere in the South. But in Charlotte, replying that I attend Temple Beth El usually causes the other person to tell me enthusiastically that my rabbi spoke at her church or his civic group.

Eventually, Rabbi Judy resigns from her pulpit, accepting an offer from a local university that includes teaching community classes and establishing a new justice center. During her last couple of years at the synagogue and her first year at Queens University of Charlotte, she and I co-author a book to guide other synagogues on their journeys of civic engagement. *Recharging Judaism* encourages congregations to step outside their buildings on issues like homelessness, engaging Jews who are more inspired by responding to injustice than by attending worship services. The book explains why this work is appropriate for synagogues and how civic engagement deepens our connection to Judaism, offering frameworks that enable a congregation to create civic change without internal divisiveness.

For three years, Rabbi Judy and I spend a couple of hours together every week, writing and editing our manuscript. Sometimes we meet in person; other weeks we work remotely with a combination of Google Docs and cellphones. I pick a unique ringtone to alert me to her calls—with a touch of irony, choosing church bells.

Once we submit the final manuscript to the publisher, our decade-plus partnership seems not actually ending, but perhaps ebbing. Our book generates a substantial calendar of speaking events across the country, but most of them enlist either her as a rabbi or me as a lay leader, not the two of us together. I reconcile myself to this new normal of weeks passing without talking to her.

The church bells chime on my cellphone several months after the manuscript goes to press. "Judy, you are not going to believe this," says Rabbi Judy. "I polled my students about how to apply their new skills in advocacy. Would you believe affordable housing is one of their top issues?"

She asks me to volunteer as the affordable housing organizer at her justice center. I always say "yes" to Rabbi Judy, a great partner and a force of nature who creates meaningful change. We collaborated on a new site for a Children's Defense Fund summer program, the first Jewish-sponsored site in the country. We produced documentaries on student diversity and affordable housing, winning two Telly awards. We co-authored our book, attracting endorsements from nationally recognized activists and winning a National Jewish Book Award.

She wants me to be a community organizer at her justice center? Yes. Of course, yes.

We created a framework in our book that we called "The Cycle of Civic Engagement." We apply this guide to our newest partnership, advocating for affordable housing under the mantle of her justice center.

Reflect. Listen. Educate. Strategize. Act. Celebrate.

Hundreds of her adult students *reflect* on lectures from civic leaders, lawyers, and educators. They choose to apply their newfound skills to the local affordable housing shortage.

We *listen* to those who show up at our launch meeting in January 2018. They pick the City Council budget and the housing bond referendum as the advocacy focus for the upcoming year.

We *educate* our volunteers about the disproportionate imbalance between housing needs and resources for the poorest among us. We train them how to communicate most effectively to City Council members.

We *strategize* to build our advocacy platform for the next City budget cycle and the upcoming housing bond referendum. We narrow our asks to four headlines with graphics on a single sheet of paper. We build power with other advocacy groups by creating a shared platform.

We *act*, connecting individually with ten of the eleven City Council members in nineteen separate appointments, often bringing representatives from other advocacy groups with us. We show up and often speak up at official government meetings.

And we win. A bigger housing bond referendum — $50 million instead of the historic $15 million. A greater share of new housing units for the lowest income households—20% instead of the usual 2%. More money for rental subsidies—$2.7 million instead of the $700,000 planned.

We *celebrate* our victories. Taking time at our meetings to bask in our collective success. Posting video clips on social media. Sharing our story on the justice center's website. Recounting anecdotes as springboards for the next advocacy cycle.

What I know about community organizing comes mostly from the research for *Recharging Judaism*. But two decades of corporate strategy consulting and sales management experience contributed skills relevant to this work—researching problems, communicating ideas and motivating people. Another decade-plus as an advocate in homelessness and affordable housing provided me with content expertise and easy access to local professionals. That personal history coalesced into successful community organizing.

Community organizing is challenging. Recruiting volunteers to show up. Training them to tell their backstories succinctly. Setting appointments with busy elected officials. Building the platform message. Practicing speaking parts with volunteers. Pivoting based on new information. Communicating with the team. Building consensus with other advocacy groups. Holding elected officials accountable. Balancing the perfect with the possible.

After we accomplished our 2018 platform goals, the 2019 affordable housing advocacy work expands to multiple issues, which require much more time. Furthermore, institutionalizing advocacy at her justice center requires shifting to paid staff, supplemented by volunteers but not solely relying on them. I tell Rabbi Judy we should start looking for my replacement.

I used to earn a living catalyzing change for businesses. My gratification stems from building something new, shepherding the business through the new normal, and then training my replacement. Take a break, and then do it again elsewhere. In my volunteer work these past sixteen years in Charlotte, I still followed this pattern—build, solidify, transition out.

Transitioning out from leading advocacy for Rabbi Judy takes another six months. We find a Presbyterian pulpit minister, an experienced community organizer able to work part-time. One of our volunteers—a military veteran, formerly homeless—becomes a paid contractor. One of our other volunteers, also now ready to lead, cuts back on his other community work to step up his time commitment. I stick around long enough for each of them to gain traction with their piece of the work and with our cadre of volunteers.

Casseroles constitute an important part of addressing homelessness. People living in shelters or lining up at soup kitchens need a hot meal. Those of us in housing possess the resources to cook for those who lack housing. We avert the crisis of hunger among the homeless when we lower housing costs so that a paycheck covers rent and meals, with enough remaining for medication, gas, and car repairs.

Casseroles serve as a gateway for many like me who choose to not only help people in the crisis of homelessness, but also to work for systems change.

As I reflect on my work, I acknowledge that organizing became all-consuming for me. I chose to sacrifice some of my personal life that year, working many evenings and weekends, even on vacation. I found politics draining, playing out political scenarios in my head at night, unable to sleep.

Yet, living my values required that I use my skills to lead in that moment, even as a volunteer. Especially as a volunteer.

The one hundred amazing people who volunteered with me kept me going. They awed me, stretching outside their comfort zones. They energized me, consistently showing up—on Queens campus, at the Government Center, and in City Council offices. They impressed me, finding their own activist voices. They empowered me, believing we could make a difference. And we did.

THE THORN
[EXCERPT]

Dee Allen.

March 19, 2003:

Coalition on Homelessness
Asked for volunteers to be
Houseless guides to visiting
Kansas University students.
I stepped forward. And I accepted their offer.
It was the easiest $50 I ever made.

For one day,
Out-of-town guests
Followed me around & took notes
Of my daily life, young and Black,
Houseless in San Francisco.

Starting point of our tour:
A protruding thorn on a stem
Called Rose Street, off upper Market.
To me, it was home.
Erin, Ben & Joe,
Midwestern, White & young
As privileged as they come
Led through labyrinthine
Corridors into oversized rooms
That could house 8 at once.

Next stop: 39 Fell.
The three Midwesterners bore
Witness to the long, sad line of desperation

I was once part of, ended at
The front registration desk inside.
Flowing like water streams, most of the day,
Shelter referrals. Vacant beds.

Next stop: Starbucks, inside the Hotel Whitcomb.
A place to get free cups of hot water.
I provided my guests with lemon tea bags
And turbinado packets.

Next stop: UN Plaza Café.
San Francisco grey sky
Began pouring cold rain.
Our crew was wet & starving.
Only dry, free area in sight:
The blue canopy above
UN Plaza Café. Closed.
Food Not Bombs huddled
Under it to serve free, hot,
Vegetarian food, as always. Soup & bread hit the spot.

Next stop: anti-war march.
The roving protest against Bush's
Planned invasion of Iraq was
Bigger than usual. Louder. Angrier.
On a whim, Erin, Ben, Joe & me
Traded one crowd for another.
We left Food Not Bombs and
Joined the march down Market,
Despite getting drenched.
Fuck the rain.
Fuck rush hour.
Time to stop a war.
Three miles in a steady
Downpour, we marched.
Through three major busy
Streets & a secondary downpour
Of chants, we marched.
Past irate cops, we marched

Against an international bloodbath
Only Fox News & PNAC wanted.

Anti-imperialist
Procession
Followed a flatbed pickup truck,
As rain continued to pour.
All banners, picket signs, voices of discontent.
The people's demand,
Shouted out loud,
Repeated the world over:
"NO WAR IN IRAQ!"

Stopover: 24th & Mission.
The procession filled in
The space between McDonald's & BART
The pickup parked in the street sideways,
Served as a temporary stage.
Three messengers with bullhorns
Delivered the same ominous news:
Bombs over Baghdad
U$ first strike
Shock & Awe
Around the world:
"THE WAR HAS BEGUN!"

Shock & Awe has spread to the Mission.
Afterwards, collective rage. That spread to me, too.
Second conflict in the Gulf. Threat on Amerikkka's
                    young.
Time to bring a war home.

Banks & PG&E
Front windows smashed
Economic damage
Fast-moving shadows
Outrace approaching cops
In the first hour of war.
I lost one of my guests,

Joe, somewhere in the raging
Anti-war procession. Erin, Ben & me
Found him, nearly snatched up
By cops eager to grab any collar.
The four of us disappeared from Mission & 22nd,
Where the first arrest was made.

Next stop: Safeway.
Like some angry wolf, my stomach growled.
Nourished on itself, with canines only I felt.
The four of us grabbed snack & dinner items.
My treat. A vegetarian panini & mango smoothie
Had my name on them. The food stamp card,
                    a lifesaver.

Back to the Thorn.
The tour ends. Full circle.
Visiting Kansas University students
Had to return to a church each night for
Their lodging, after a day with their houseless guides.
But not Erin, Ben & Joe. These three Jayhawks
Were so intrigued with my massive squat. I gave them
A room with a sliding glass patio-style door, 2
Floodlights mounted to the upper wall & a
Working microwave on the floor.
Somewhere they could warm food, dine & sleep.
Now they had plenty to write papers about—

ADD A LITTLE COLOR FOR JUSTICE

Sandra Hall

"You gotta take the training San, you'll see. You gotta do this." For the most part of the five years that my friend Pam and I coordinated an Annual Health Fair for the 3rd Legislative District in Illinois, she was persistent in sharing her excitement about the Restorative Justice (RJ) work she was involved in around the city, state, and country.

"This is a good fit for you," she nudged.

I was mostly hesitant about the prospect of getting into the RJ training during that time as I was between jobs and barely working 10 hours a week. I was concerned that my salary really couldn't handle the $500 price tag that accompanied the training. To counter my defense, Pam shared with me there was possibly a scholarship available. I completed the application and submitted it as needed.

Several weeks later, I had an opportunity to take the four-day Restorative Justice Circle Keeper training. I didn't have to make any promises, sign any contracts, or promise to repay by a certain deadline. I completed the application and simply told my truth; I couldn't afford the tuition. The social worker part of me felt guilty for taking the scholarship that someone else could use.

That was over fifteen years ago. That four-day training changed my life. My trainer was a phenomenal woman by the name of Ora Schub. She, along with Cheryl Graves, founded the Community Youth Justice Institute (CJYI) in Chicago. Both attorneys-turned-R-J-practitioners had trained and learned so much from hundreds of others in their restorative work around the country and the world. Upon completion, I made a commitment to myself to take advantage of every opportunity to utilize the new skills I had learned and committed to ensuring that as an RJ practitioner/Circle Keeper, I was going to pass along the gifts of RJ and share with others as much as I possibly could. My friend Pamela Purdie has been an integral part of the CJYI family, and I have had the privilege of sitting in circle with Pam, Cheryl, and Ora before she made her transition (Summer 2018) and learned so much from each of them. That journey continues with Pam and Cheryl.

This is how Restorative Justice (RJ) is defined on the CJYI website.

Restorative Justice is a theory of justice that emphasizes repairing the harm caused by crime and conflict. It places decisions in the hands of those who have been most affected by a wrongdoing, and gives equal concern to the victim, the offender, and the surrounding community. Restorative responses to crime and conflict, such as peace-making circles, are designed to repair the harm, heal broken relationships, and address the underlying reasons for the offense.

Restorative justice emphasizes the importance of both individual accountability and collective accountability. Individuals are responsible for choices they make resulting in harm to others, but collectives at the neighborhood, city, county, state and national level are responsible for social conditions which increase the likelihood of crime. Crime and conflict generate opportunities to build community and increase grassroots power when restorative practices are employed.

Peacemaking Circles
The primary restorative practice used by the Community Justice for Youth Institute is peace-making circles. The circle is a process that brings together individuals who wish to engage in conflict resolution, healing, support, decision making or other activities in which honest communication, relationship development, and community building are core desired outcomes.

A few months after completing the RJ training, I joined the RJ community at my church in Chicago. From there I was able to participate in RJ work in my church, my church-wide community, and the community at large. I have been able to use the skills in schools, churches, private and not-for-profits, and community-based organizations; with children, adults and seniors, male, female, and co-ed groups. I've incorporated RJ in many things in parenting, teen, and youth groups alike.

As a trained social worker, educator, and consultant, I have been an advocate for hundreds of children and families for over 40 years.

Sometimes the outcries were for my colleagues and me, directed toward the injustices within the various systems in which I was employed. I have raised my voice and spoken out oftentimes when it wasn't popular, was not appreciated by the powers that be, and have been labeled "a troublemaker." As a single parent, I have had to raise my hand, take on responsibilities I didn't necessarily want to do, advocate for myself and my child—to ensure we gained access to, didn't get excluded from, skipped over and/or cut out of programs or whatever was going on in our community.

As a social worker, I have worked in a variety of settings: mental health, health care, early child development, school-age programs, and child welfare. More importantly, I believe I was called and trained to speak out and speak up for myself, to agitate situations in general when I didn't fit the box or when the "business as usual" protocol didn't work for me. Sometimes I had to leave a system (quit a job) in order to be a more meaningful advocate from outside of the system.

My mom taught me by example to speak up for myself. I vividly recall my mother arguing with the store clerk if they shortchanged her a nickel or even two pennies—making sure her opinion was considered with my dad or other adults. What was interesting though is that when I mirrored what I was learning, it wasn't always fondly received. At five years old, I protested the idea of being told I would be wearing the same outfit for Easter as my three sisters (two older and one younger). "At least get my dress in a different color," was my request. Another example was my response to being told while in 8th grade, that I was expected to attend the same high school as my four older siblings. I begged, did a little research and requested to attend a school not too far from our home. My biggest issue was simply the fact that all my siblings had previously attended that school. In both situations, after a short time, my parents acquiesced. A light blue dress instead of the green dress my sisters had was purchased for me, and I was able to attend the high school of my choice.

Last year, I was able to participate with an RJ program that collaborated with a Chicago-area community organization that takes monthly bus rides to a downstate women's prison. In August 2018, I joined the organization for this journey. This was my first time going inside a prison. In my role as a social worker and an RJ practitioner, I had been inside local jails and a juvenile detention center, but never a prison. Three months later I was hired to work part-time with this organization and since late November 2018, I now coordinate the Reunification Ride program. After a few visits, I noticed how impersonal the space felt and thought about adding some bright colors to the big gymnasium to enhance the visiting experience for incarcerated moms, their children, guardians, and other family members.

What I've learned over the past 15 years is that being restorative is a choice and it's a lifestyle. Being exposed to RJ work has taught me how to be restorative in ALL my relationships. Breaking through systems that are so embedded and committed to punishing people (prisons, schools, etc.) as opposed to restorative practices takes a lot of work and it's a process. Breaking down those barriers to being restorative can happen and is happening.

Having a restorative classroom in a big school can be so much more effective if the whole school is committed to restorative practices. Many schools in the Chicago area and across the country that utilize restorative practices have incorporated 'peace rooms' that are decorated by staff and students in bright and soft colors, affirmations, signs, pictures, comfy pillows, chairs, items and artifacts that have meaning and value to that community. Peace circles take place in these spaces also. The peace rooms create a safe space for students and staff to go to release, reconnect and reenergize, get the support they need to take the next step, to repair harm caused. Peace rooms are welcoming spaces.

One of my current projects for advocacy involves infusing brightly colored walls to enhance the monthly visiting experience in the multi-purpose gymnasium in the downstate Illinois women's prison I visit monthly.

Incarceration separates children from their parents, creating a huge loss for all parties involved, impacts their daily lives and in many cases, incarceration creates more problems than it intends to solve. If the incarcerated parent is the breadwinner and the custodial parent, it creates a financial loss and children being displaced from their homes, schools, and community activities they may be involved in; a shift in the financial responsibilities to other family members and/or the state.

In the regular visiting room, moms and their families share

snacks and other food from the vending machines, which they have to pay for, share close space with other moms who are incarcerated and their family members, and, most importantly, are able to touch and hug loved ones, but only sparingly.

Visits in the gymnasium with the Reunification Ride (RR) program, allow family members to touch, give and receive hugs, play table games, some floor games, jump rope, play with balls, play basketball, draw and color in coloring books/construction paper, make cards, enjoy treats and activities that coincide with national holidays, share a lunch together prepared by the facility, read stories together, and have family photos taken to capture their time together. A copy of the pictures taken are sent to the family members and the moms inside generally within 30 days after the monthly visit. Transportation is also provided for Chicago-area children and their guardians, and the entire day, which includes at least a three-hour visit, is entirely free to the moms and their families.

While visits in the gymnasium are less-guarded than the visiting room, it is a gymnasium that's big and impersonal, non-welcoming, not well insulated nor air-conditioned, has poor lighting, dingy tan bricks and white walls. I envision an infusion of bright colored walls to start the creation of a more welcoming space. Next, I envision creating smaller more intimate areas within that space and/or identifying and possibly utilizing other spaces within the correctional facility for moms with smaller children to be able to play on the floor with them; or just smaller more intimate spaces for moms and their children to talk privately, read stories, and just be together. I also envision these spaces furnished with bright colorful lights, punctuated with colorful area rugs, a variety of books, toys and activities with moms and their children immersed, enjoying and learning with and from each other.

I have shared my vision for enhancing this space verbally and in writing with my supervisor, and our contact person inside the facility. I have previously participated in days of providing service to local schools and community-based organizations that included surface and intense cleaning projects, sorting, organizing spaces, disposing of papers, boxes and garbage and yes, painting. Painting walls, furniture and murals. So, I envisioned engaging a group of my family members, friends and colleagues, getting them to commit their time and money to pay for the paint, related supplies, bus rental and/or gas for cars to transport us to the downstate correctional facility and together physically create a more welcoming visiting space. My response from our contact inside was that the prison will not allow a group of outsiders to come in and paint the gymnasium, but they will accept donations of paint and supplies to decorate the gymnasium.

I am in the process of exploring the possible use of another space within the facility that I understand is used for only a few days during the summer for a "Mommy and Me" camp as a possible option for our RR monthly visits. I have signed up to participate in the 2020 Mommy & Me camp myself so I can see first-hand what it looks like. I have also identified a group of nearly one-hundred committed people who have pledged to make financial commitments of at least $20 to help transform the gymnasium, to make it a more welcoming space for the monthly RR visits with moms. Additionally, I want to identify a way to engage the moms inside, and some of their adult family members, all of whom are important members of this community; to get them on board to assist in advocacy efforts around transforming the gymnasium, and/or identifying an entirely different space.

The moms have been quite vocal about other programs. They often verbalize their appreciation of this RR program during our individual encounters with them and their families. Both groups consistently express appreciation of the RR in our goodbye circle at the end of each monthly visit. Mothers can begin by identifying the colors to paint the walls, creating affirmations, and infusing their voices in the conversation as to what the new transformed visiting space should look like. Hopefully the new welcoming space for enhancing monthly visits will be completed one paintbrush stroke at a time by Christmas 2020.

PATHWAYS

Jarrett Mazza

I was told by my mother right before she died that I should have taken more of an interest in my community. How do you define what a community is? I didn't know. At the time, I tried to define it because it was something I had never really thought of, not until I realized that I didn't have one, not in the traditional sense of the word.

"You don't care about anything! That's your problem!" My ex-girlfriend, Cathy, shouted this before she left. She was blonde, had a decent paying job, and spent most of her time working as a copy editor, all day at a desk as a corporate drone, moving a lot, but thinking about very little. Who the hell was she to lecture me about not doing enough when all she did was read words that other people have written? She wasn't a humanitarian or a community leader or someone who went out of their way to make a positive impact on someone else's life.

In the end, she was the same as I was. Aware, but not entirely there.

"Me! What the hell do you do?!"

I rolled my eyes. I told her that I didn't care about anything she said or did, and that I was going to start a group to help the kids who had it rough and who, like me, were heading down the wrong path. I planned to have it at the local library. My sense of altruism, which I felt this was, had only risen so sharply because I had accepted the truth about who I was: a regular guy, who lived and worked a regular job, and who finally came to see himself as less than he ever was before. I was worse because I had yet to embrace that terrible reality which I couldn't escape from, a reality so many see so often, a simple yet daunting revelation: nothing to fight for, and it's time I do something about it.

When I was younger, I used to think that if I screamed or decided to hammer my head into the wall, someone would hear. Sometimes,

I think I'd have to shoot a gun because experiencing that pain wasn't enough. Parents were there, but they were never attentive, not to the details, and the details were where the answers lay.

Regardless of where I was, I always wanted to be somewhere that wasn't here. I envisioned this entirely new person, like I didn't grow into the man I was today. I tried to figure that the world wasn't as sad as I made it out to be. I used to steal and yet, I didn't want to call myself a thief. A thief implies you steal goods, and other valuables with the added interest of selling them in order to make money. I never stole anything I wanted to sell or, for that matter, wanted to keep for myself.

I liked cars because I liked how fast they went. I stole them from people who had too many. Two friends and I would loiter outside a packed parking garage connected to an office building where men and women who wore suits would work. There were rules in the garage. Sometimes we had to pretend that we were who we said we were, workers and such. When we were given the opportunity, together, we would break into the cars, and take them for joyrides before returning them later. It was fun until it wasn't, until we'd get busted doing our twelfth stint, and were reprimanded by a man who had big hands, who socked me in the back of the skull, and sent me straight to the floor.

"What the hell do you think you're doing?"

I didn't have an answer. He punched me again, and the cops came, pressed charges. As I sat in that lonely, stinky jail cell, with blood gushing from my nose, and being in the company of drug dealers, drunks, and hookers, everything came to light. I was a guy who lost so often that I forgot what it felt like to win. The judge sentenced me to community service, and I was ordered to complete a number of hours, pick up garbage and clean graffiti off jungle gyms and sidewalks. When doing this one day, I spotted a boy sitting alone by one of the slides. I couldn't guess his age, or maybe I just didn't want to. I was about the same age as the kid when I started to walk out of line. I used to think I was doing it because I liked it. I guess I was just doing it. I wanted to get out and make my life better than it was. I knew it wasn't the way to do it. I didn't care until I realized that I had to.

There's a feeling you get when you know you've hit rock bottom. Granted, I thought I had always been at the bottom, but this wasn't the bottom. This was the space underneath the soil, the place where everything is cold, and it feels wet even though it's really dry. You are sinking and yet, you aren't falling. You're awake but you feel like you've been asleep for half your life. You sit alone and wonder why there's no one there with you. You look around, hoping to find someone who will tell you where everything went bad, the time when you slipped from the path that is supposed to lead to a good, healthy life. I never thought about the future when I was too young to consider the implications of all of my choices.

You have this image of yourself, like you're nothing, and that you were born into nothingness. I wanted to walk in circles and approach a window and jump through the fucking glass. You want to be better and you keep seeing yourself as someone who knows the path to redemption, how you could find it if only there was someone to help you to get there. You blame yourself and your community, then you blame yourself, and your parents too.

Later, I walked up to a new arrival, a kid, and I asked him where he was from, where his parents were, and what he was doing asleep in the park. His parents didn't care. They left him for reasons that I didn't care to discover. My life was shit. I didn't want it to be this way and I had to break the cycle, and now I could, if I chose to.

What was the one thing about the world that I hated and wished I could change?

If I were ever to have one of those "your-life-is-a-mess-and-it's-time-to-fix-your-shit" moments, this was it. So, I spent the next six months trying to organize something where I could bring the kids who needed help off the street and into "a safe space." This was something I heard more than once. When I was there, I remembered helping some people who said that's what they needed. I never focused on what it meant to be in a place where you were protected, and where you didn't have to feel afraid of anything or anyone.

"This space?" said the elderly woman at the library. "Does it work for you?"

I was in a room with big windows and steel chairs stacked in a corner. In my hands, I had a list of names on a sign-up sheet that I managed to create with the help of child protection services. There were six names on it. I created a Facebook group and before any of this even began, I wondered about myself more than I did about any of the other children. What on earth could I *possibly* provide to them that other people didn't *already* try to give? I was as much of a problem as they were. I was told by one my teachers that if I didn't try to stop myself from making the same mistakes, I would grow up to be a menace to society. I would transform into one of those assholes that did nothing but increase the crime rate and heighten the levels of stupidity currently being pumped out like gasoline. Whatever, I thought. You don't know me. As it turned out, they kind of did.

"This space…it'll work just fine," I said to the librarian.

She was elderly, had a handkerchief tucked into her pocket, with big glasses on her face.

"I'm glad."

I was about to say, "I'm glad too" as in 'I'm so very glad that you're here.' Honestly, I didn't know. In my mind, I kept on picturing all these frazzled, vagabond children strolling in off the street, with all this pent-up hostility, and buried fury that they decided to let out onto me. I think they thought that I was going to be like everyone else that tried to help them in their community. And, then a kid came in, no older than ten, alone, and with one of those flyers that I handed out back at the center. It was rolled up into his palm.

"Hi," he said, timid, reserved, not knowing what to say.

He was obviously nervous about being there. I was too.

"Hi?"

"Is this…" The boy had a difficult time speaking, so I walked closer, knowing that by being too far I was only increasing his level of uncertainty. "The youth assistance program?"

I squinted and looked away for just a second. 'The circle for sharing stories' was not something that I thought I would find myself affiliated with, but I remembered what I wrote on the flyer, my words.

"Yes," I replied. "Yes. This is exactly what that is. What's your name?"

The boy looked at me with sullen eyes, mopey because he didn't know what to expect.

"Casey. My name's Casey."

"Casey," I said, pretending to be all teacher-like and cool, knowing fully well that what I was, wasn't much. "I'm Brian. Nice to meet you."

He smiled. I shook his hand, like an adult should do whenever he meets someone new, and I again slipped into that teacher mentality where, if you would have said it to me fifteen years ago, I would have said you had lost your mind. Me? Teaching? No way. In the end, I think, we're all waiting to teach someone something.

It took me some time to know what I wanted to instill. More kids came later, all of them pretty much the same, and when they were gathered, I sat in the circle the same as they did. I finally had my answer. I wanted to talk. I hated talking. People exchanging feelings, discussing shared experiences, the past choices we regret, and what we seek to change.

Dialogue was a word that I thought was defined only by speech, usually when referencing a film or the conversations among characters. Really, what it meant was just talking until you learned something or you managed to grow. The kid was young. If anyone had the opportunity to grow, it was him. For me, I always thought it was too late.

"So," I said, to all the kids sitting around in the circle, patiently waiting for someone to say something. I was glad it was me who decided to do so. "Who would like to talk first?"

Many hands shot up, and the room got a little dark. I turned on all the lights until I could see every single one.

AFTER THE ELECTION

Allene Nichols

They are vulnerable, my students,
children of immigrants
and children of entitlement alike,
sitting in tidy rows, looking at each other
from the corners of their eyes.

One blond-haired, blue-eyed boy
who longs to leave this community
and its college for a university and
a fraternity, asks, "Don't you think
it's going to be great to have
Donald Trump as our president?"

The room draws in a sharp breath.
This is too new. They don't know how
to be themselves after this morning's news.
The quiet girl in the front row, her skin
and voice whispering Mexico;
the queer girl with the blue hair
and defiant punk hair spikes;
The transgender man, still trying
to reconcile with his own skin.
They all hold their breath.

I think to myself, this blue-eyed boy
is still a fetus, unformed and unaware,
a parrot of his parents' fears.
But the others are truly afraid:
the girl whose Vietnamese-American father
was told to "go back to China"
when he stopped to pick up doughnuts

on his way to work this morning;
the Muslim girl whose friend's headscarf
was thrown in the lake at lunch;
and the others, trying hard to save themselves
by closing around their thoughts and feelings,
young flowers turning back into buds.

In this class, we learn how to make
arguments, and they will follow the clues
and make strong arguments, but only
if this moment of fear, of difference,
does not wrench their courage from them.

It is I, the queer professor, the woman
professor, who must reply.
"I think this president will be good
for straight white men," I say.
The boy does not look away.
Nor do I. And the students let out
a collective sigh. There will be battles
to fight, I tell them. Let us start with
our words. Let us tell the truth,
even when it would be easier
to hide.

POEM TO MY BROTHER, JOSE BELLO*

A. J. Chilson

I stand with my brother, Jose Bello,
And speak against what I find to be low.

What I find is second-class mistreatment,
And decent people facing harassment.

I find the person behind the cruel deeds
Is a wealthy rogue with an evil bleed.

And this rouge has his Nazi-like henchmen
Tearing away men, women and children.

For them, life without clean water, good food,
And toilet paper is, safe to say, crude.

It is only fitting that some meet death,
Without having had one nice freedom breath.

People like that wealthy rogue bring great shame,
And the country I once loved a bad name.

*In honor of the poet deported after publicly reciting a poem criticizing the US immigration system

71

GENDER EQUITY

JUSTICE

I THINK OF LYN LIFSHIN

Laura Sweeney

I think of Lyn Lifshin

and wonder why I can't
give myself permission
to write, revise, submit,
revolt!
While Lyn Lifshin scribbles
a tango across the Poetry Super
Highway, writing odes to Marilyn
and Malala, where are the other
women writers?
Why aren't they publishing?
Thinking of Lyn Lifshin
and her Mad Girl poems,
I am the mad woman
in the Charleston Hotel
wondering what persona I should take.
Could I make a name for myself
like Lyn Lifshin,
Queen of the Small Press?
But I panic at the dilemma — —
does my poem go in *Feminist Studies*
or the *Evening Street Review*?
When words are your life,
placement matters;
the declaration of independence
a woman writer makes:
I will not be silenced.
I will not make sense.
I will rage like riotous scarlet,
subtle to the bone.

I will think of Lyn Lifshin,
put my head down,
and write my way into
epiphany.

HOOKED

Anne Farrer Scott

The pussyhat is a symbol of support and solidarity for women's rights and political resistance. Make a hat! Give a hat! Wear your hat! Share a hat! (pussyhatproject.com)

"Mom, do you still crochet?"
My daughter wanted a pussyhat.
I hadn't held a crochet hook in years.
My daughter wanted to march and protest.
How could I say no?
What to do? And how to do it?
First, find the Pussyhat Project.

Knitting and crochet are traditionally women's crafts, and we want to celebrate these arts… Anything handmade shows a level of care, and we care about women's rights, so it is appropriate to symbolize this march with a handmade item, one made with a skill that has been passed down from woman to woman for generations. (pussyhatproject.com)

As a young woman, I refused to sew, knit, crochet, because needlework was what women were supposed to do. I wanted to live outside societal expectations. No strings would tie me down, or so I thought.

But when I was fraught and knotted in my twenties, a wise old Quaker woman told me: "Work with wool."

I did, although I was never what you would call adventurous with yarn. Actually, I was somewhere south of craft and never quite achieved what patterns termed "the instant heirloom." I was always relieved when all that looping turned out as it was supposed to. "The lyf so short, the craft so long to lerne," Chaucer knew.

I made baby blankets, doll dresses, Christmas stockings (twice—

mice ate the first ones). A soft green carrier for my daughter's Cabbage Patch doll that—just as the pattern promised—looked exactly like a cabbage (albeit an enormous, floppy cabbage). A granny square afghan for my wise Quaker friend and a granny square sweater for my mother.

> *The more we are seen, the more we are heard. Let's come together to support women's rights in a creative and impactful way.* (pussyhatproject.com)

I certainly wanted to support women's rights—mine, my daughter's, and my granddaughter's. First, I needed to find a pattern—definitely not with ears to attach or intricate stitching. Online there were all sorts, many beyond me. Finally, I found one I thought I could manage.

> *To fit an average adult head. It's very stretchy, so will fit a range of sizes. And it's easy to adjust: make the ribbing sections shorter or longer ... to fit smaller or larger heads, respectively.* (kimwerker.com)

The pattern was for a half-double crochet that lay flat with the sides stitched together and corners that perked into kitty ears. This might be possible...

> *Yarn of any weight in a sufficient amount to complete the hat, and an appropriately sized hook.*

I would use a larger hook (N or P), but who knew how many shades of pink there could be? Rose, hot pink, dusty pink, raspberry, bubblegum...

> *First Ribbing Section: Make a chain slightly longer than 4" (10 cm). Work in sc-blo ribbing.*
> *Second Ribbing Section: Make as First Ribbing Section but do not fasten off.*

"Grab them by the pussy," Trump had said—definitely motivation to resurrect an old skill—a very old skill. After many flubs, many mistakes, and much unraveling and doing over, I finally get the hang of it.

Middle Section: Ch 2, rotate 90 degrees to crochet across the ribbed edge. Placing your stitches consistently as you go, HDC in each row-edge across. Repeat HDC Row until piece measures about 17" from bottom edge of ribbing, fasten off.

And then the doing, the making. At last, I settle into the comfortable old looping motion. Entwined in those loops are wisps of memory. Holding my children when they seemed to weigh no more than a bag of potato chips. My small son asking: How does God make clouds? How does God make people? How does God get into people? My frustrated young daughter wanting to know: Do you have to be a kid first to grow up?

Finishing: Layer First Ribbing Section behind Middle Section, lining up on long edge of the ribbing with the last row of HDC. Holding both pieces together and working through both thicknesses at the same time, with a yarn needle sew the two sections together using whipstitch. When you get to the end, fasten off. Fold the hat in half so the ribbing sections are lined up. Whipstitch the two sides of the hat together (or use whichever seaming technique you prefer), keeping the bottom edge of the ribbing open — that's where you'll put your head!

Finally, I finish a pussyhat for my daughter. Then I continue. I stitch hats for two of her friends. Then a dear friend of mine, and my granddaughter.

The pussyhats done, I want to keep on going, keep on looping: Shawls! Scarves! Ponchos!

So now, again, I work with wool. Well, mostly acrylic. A grandma torquing granny squares. Starting with an empty, lonely hook and chaining, looping, stitching *something*.

Research shows that crocheting and knitting do relieve stress and promote good health. Heart rate and blood pressure drop. Cortisol levels fall, and dopamine levels rise. The brain's reward center perks up. Neural connections connect. Mood improves.

That was before the Trump administration.

If ever I had a narrative thread, I have lost it. Now, while I binge watch breaking—broken—news on cable TV, I crochet for dear life. "Very fine people" marching in Charlottesville. "Shithole countries." "Beautiful barbed wire." Pangs of my rage and unending despair work their way into each shawl, scarf, poncho.

I stitch too tightly. It's not the gentle, soothing motion I once knew. I fiercely work the yarn. I'm not looping so much as jabbing and yanking. Highly strung, I end up with a shawl so stiff it has the heft of a doorstop. The results are no longer soft and cozy. It turns out I am making body armor here.

But I keep pulling loop through loop, making what I can. Again, Chaucer knew: "Lies, tears and needlework the Lord will give/In kindness to us women as we live."

Weave in loose ends.

All sorts of things can be—have been—crocheted. Grass (front and back loop single crochet with avocado and sage yarn). Our very cells—nucleus, cytoplasm, mitochondria. A brain with spinal cord descending. A neuron with axons and dendrites. The human heart.

Pondering my empty hook, I wonder whether a world could be crocheted. Perhaps a half double crochet for the bright, blue sky. A chevron stitch for the ripples of the river. Tight, single crochet for the dry sand. Floating, bobbled clouds. Triple crochet for the trunks of trees. A thin yarn for the leaves. A finer yarn for the tiny people struggling to cross the rippling river.

And in this world, children won't be separated from their parents.

THE BIRTH OF HEALING AND ACTIVISM

Greta McClain

On a hot July night in 2017, my life was forever changed. As I walked through a parking lot, I felt his hands gripping my wrists tighter and tighter as he pinned me against the hood of my car. I lost all sense of who I was. It was the night I lost all hope and my will to continue.

An experience like this would devastate most anyone. The physical wounds — the bruises, the black eye, the cuts and scrapes — they heal over time. The emotional wounds linger and fester. A poison began to spread, infecting not only my mind but my spirit as well. As the disease wove its way through my psyche, I fell deeper and deeper into despair. There was no relief for my pain, no reprieve to my suffering; or so I thought. As I finished writing my goodbye letters and reviewed the plan I had made to end my life, a miracle happened. It was a miracle from the most unlikely source, but it was a miracle nonetheless.

I was waiting, making sure everyone would be at work when I slipped the goodbye letter into their mailbox. My mind, poisoned as it was, knew I would be in no shape to try to offer an excuse if I were caught. I couldn't tolerate my pain any longer and I was not about to risk someone keeping me from completing my mission. As I lay in the darkness I stared at my phone, watching the minutes slowly tick away. I had only watched for maybe two minutes, but seemed like a lifetime. I still had a little over three hours before I could deliver the letters. The waiting was excruciating. I finally picked up my phone, and that is when it happened. That is when my life was changed once again.

Alyssa Milano had posted a retweet on Twitter. It was a short, but immensely powerful post that included a little hashtag called #MeToo. That post had quickly spread across social media and thousands, no, tens of thousands of people were saying #MeToo. It was in that moment I felt the birth of my healing process. It was then I saw the faint glimmer of hope. I experienced my miracle.

The recovery would be difficult, but for the first time in months I was willing to try. I drank in the medicine of hope and inspiration I found in a social media hashtag, and the healing slowly began to flow through my veins. Just as a broken bone oftentimes heals and becomes stronger, my mind and spirit became stronger with each passing day. I began feeling whole again, and for the first time in months I felt I had a reason to continue. As my wounds healed and I found myself getting stronger and stronger, I had a revelation. Just as a Twitter post born out of pain and evil had saved my life, perhaps my suffering could somehow help others as well. Maybe, just maybe, my story could bring a sense of hope and healing to someone. If it helped just one person, then perhaps my suffering had been worth it.

When I felt I was strong enough, I made my decision. When I was confident my voice, like the voice of Alyssa Milano, had power, I decided to turn my nightmare into a catalyst for good. I decided to share the horror I had experienced — and my journey to recovery — with a total stranger.

I sent a Facebook message to Women's March Tennessee detailing my story. I did not hold much hope that I would get a response, but I found putting my rape into words was therapeutic — even empowering. Even though I was sending intimate details of the worst day of my life to an unknown person, someone I would probably never meet, I somehow felt more confident. I could not have explained the exact feeling or the reason for the feeling if my life had depended on it. All I knew was I felt stronger. I felt less self-conscious.

I felt like me again.

The surprise I felt when I actually got a response is indescribable. The fact that this total stranger actually read what I wrote and took the time to respond was validation that my story did matter, that my voice was important. However, when I began to read the message, I started thinking it had been sent to the wrong person.

Women's March Tennessee was holding a conference the morning before the 2018 march. The message was an invitation to be a co-organizer and facilitator for the #MeToo caucus. I read those couple of sentences over and over until I was finally convinced the message was indeed meant for me. It was an honor I certainly was not expecting, and an invitation that was absolutely terrifying. It was one thing to write down the words. It was another thing to actually share the words with some unknown, invisible person on social media. It was something totally different to stand in front of actual living, breathing people and talk about the most horrific moment of my life.

I stared at that message for what seemed like hours, paralyzed with fear, uncertainty, and even excitement. I don't remember typing. I don't remember what I said. And I don't remember hitting the send button. What I do remember is the panic I felt when I realized I had just agreed to help organize and speak at the #MeToo caucus. What was I thinking? It wasn't all that long ago I was just a few hours from killing myself. Now I was going to stand and tell my story to a room full of people I had never met? What the hell was I thinking?

After finally catching my breath, I slowly began to calm myself down. I knew anyone attending a Women's March would be an ally. I knew anyone attending the conference and selecting the #MeToo caucus would be at least sympathetic and gentle if I totally bombed.

To my surprise, the caucus not only went very well, I received a lot of encouragement and even some praise. That was the spark I needed to continue sharing my story. It was the spark which ignited the fire that extinguished any doubt or hesitation. That fire eventually erupted into an unquenchable thirst to help other survivors find the same empowerment I had found. It also led to me starting a small grassroots organization called Silent No Longer Tennessee. It is run by survivors who want to help their fellow survivors find their voice; to feel the liberating freedom and empowerment it can bring. Our ultimate goal is to raise enough money to obtain our 501(c)4 and become a full-time advocacy organization that provides creative opportunities for survivors to share their stories.

Silent No Longer TN has also helped me continue to heal and find empowerment through the inspiring courage and strength of others. In February of 2019, we held a rally outside the Tennessee State Capitol to protest Representative David Byrd. He had recently been named the chair of the Education Administration Subcommittee even though three women had come forward and accused him of sexually molesting them when he was their high school basketball coach. He was named the chair even though he has never once denied the allegations made against him, and even after an audio tape of him apologizing to one of his victims was released.

Being raped by a complete stranger in a parking lot nearly cost me my life. What the mental anguish and trauma of being sexually molested by someone you trust and admire does to the psyche of a fifteen-year-old is beyond my comprehension. What I did comprehend was the need for survivors, advocates, activists, and everyday people to stand up and make it clear that this was NOT acceptable. We began attending the subcommittee meetings whenever possible, and, shortly afterwards, a volunteer with Enough is Enough Tennessee messaged me. She asked if we would be interested in partnering with them in the fight to remove Byrd from office. I jumped at the chance and I am incredibly thankful I did.

That partnership gave me the opportunity to meet one of the women who found the courage to speak out against Byrd. Watching her calmly and confidently reveal her nightmare in front of friends, strangers, and the media is nothing short of amazing. It was so inspirational and powerful it made her seem almost superhuman. Watching the commitment and energy these social justice warrior women showed is beyond words. Simply being in their presence has given me the stamina and drive to push on despite the many setbacks we have experienced. It has broadened my vision, creativity, and drive to reach further than I had ever dreamed before. The experience even led me to write two legislative bills and find the confidence to approach lawmakers and invite them to sponsor the bills.

My rape may have nearly ended by life, but it also resurrected me. It has provided me the chance to utilize my skills for the betterment of my community and re-energized my passion for writing. The partnership also allowed me to improve my community organizing skills, which has led to powerful vigils, energetic rallies, and an expansion of awareness.

Women and men who had never considered being an activist, who never even had a desire to attend a rally, have told me they are educating themselves. They are looking past the headlines and diving into the specifics. They are calling and emailing lawmakers, attending rallies, and learning how to become organizers in their communities. In short, my life-altering experience actually transformed me into a stronger, more determined woman who helped others find their passion as well. It has proven to me that Margaret Meade was correct when she said a small group of strong, committed citizens can indeed change the world—or at least their little corner of the world.

STANDING LONG ENOUGH TO MOURN

Hunter Liguore

Sunday afternoon. Cars cluster at the traffic lights on the corner of Main Street and Dowd Avenue. Patches of snow bank the gazebo on the Canton town green, which rests between the two roads. Maple trees line the sidewalk, their stark branches stretch to the pale January sky. In the summer, the green might host a bandstand or a craft fair. But as drivers approach the *Welcome* sign, they might be surprised to see a different spectacle—a line of still, silent women. They appear to be almost meditating or praying; they are dressed completely in black: hats, heavy coats, winter boots, gloves, scarves—all black.

Canton, Connecticut is a cozy, wooded community in the Farmington Valley region, around 20 minutes from the state capital. It boasts heavily treed mountains on all sides, and plenty of trails for hikers. It made its name as a manufacturing town in 1826 with the inception of the Collins Company known for its durable axes. By 1856, the company was the largest producer of edged tools. Today, the neighborhood maintains its small-town appearance with the help of family-owned businesses, like the antique shop across the street from the green. Only within the last eight years did a corporate-dominated shopping center open at the edge of town about five minutes away.

The women stand in silence. The traffic moves around them. Some honk. Many stare, as if trying to assess what it means. No banner announces why they are here. One would have to walk up and ask, like two joggers did, and then a mother and daughter out on an afternoon stroll. As a flyer is passed out, a short discussion ensues. "We are grieving. We're here to mourn the violence in the world."

The group takes their name from a worldwide network called "Women in Black," which serves to connect women with others in the name of promoting peace in opposition to violence. While the network cannot be certain how many groups exist worldwide, they do post vigils from varied places such as: North Ireland, Azerbaijan, Canada, Germany, India, Israel, Italy, and more.

As Susan Jorgensen, one of the women standing, relates, "I stand because I can. I stand to support the countless people throughout the world who have been wounded, who have lost a loved one to violence. I lament. I mourn. I am deeply grieved."

Part of standing means doing something in the name of change. As one member, who wished to remain anonymous, explains, "When we mourn, we often begin in a place of denial and move to a place of acceptance. Through acceptance comes understanding, and with understanding we are given the opportunity to move on to something else." In this case, the "something else" is a world where violence, in its various degrees, takes a backseat to peace.

"When I stand," Susan says, "I can make a difference, even if the difference is a random comment or nod made by a nameless passenger in a car."

The Sunday gathering, which began mid-January, and will continue throughout the 2013 year, came not long after the reporting of the Newtown school shooting. Newtown lies to the west of Canton, around forty-five minutes by highway, a tragedy that has gained national attention, spurring a variety of protests against gun laws and violence. But the weekly vigil, explains Leslie Gordon, a local yoga teacher, isn't just about Newtown. "Newtown was a catalyst, but it is bigger than one event. It's about our deep grief around violence in the world, our world—our children's world." She questions, "What kind of a world are we nurturing for our children?"

Claudette Baril, one of the contact members for the group, adds, "We're here as a reminder that life is changing for lots of people. We're not under the illusion that it won't change for us. We're *each* responsible for *all* our children."

As the traffic continues to pulse by, and the gray mist lifts off the adjacent mountain, the women become statuesque in the winter cold. But you can hardly tell that their fingertips and toes are chilled, because they stand so still, so poised and meditative. In the quiet, between the traffic lull, there is a strange power in witnessing these women, who vary in age. Some are mothers, grandmothers — all are daughters. They come from different towns, different backgrounds and occupations. Some meet for the first time.

Not more than twenty minutes into the vigil, a local police officer pulls up on the icy lawn, red and blue lights flashing, calling attention to them. The women stir slightly from their stoic positions. One or two wonder if they'll be driven off. "Are we being arrested," whispers one middle-aged woman to the next.

The officer relates that he was sent by his supervisor to find out why they are there. "You're not doing anything wrong," he assures. The fact that he's come is evidence that word has traveled in the small town. One can imagine the calls being made: "There's something happening on the green," or "There are a bunch of women dressed in black — can you send someone to check it out?" Maybe it's a sign of stricter vigilance, to nip any perceived danger or eruptions before they escalate. In post-Newtown Connecticut, anything out of the ordinary is cause for alarm. But as the officer learns — and the town soon enough — this gathering is far from stirring up trouble. In fact, it's quite the opposite.

"We stand for an end to acts of violence." Claudette invites the officer to take a flyer, and innocently says, "You know about the violence?"

There is a slight pause from the officer, then he nods, "Yes, of course."

Claudette tells him they will be out here every Sunday. A handshake is exchanged, and before long, the cruiser departs. The traffic, which slowed to a greater degree — with lots of rubbernecking — starts to return to normal. The women don't discuss the visit, but resume their prayers in silence, heads lowered, like participants at a funeral.

In speaking individually to the dozen or more women, it's clear each brings a slightly different reason why they are moved to stand, although they are unified. "For me," explains Nora Jamieson, a Canton resident and psychotherapist, "Women in Black conjures the powerful image in our psyches of women in mourning — not one woman, but a collective of women, who have always had a particular relation to life. Women bring life in; we nurture life. Mourning women remind us of what and who has been harmed as a result of how we conduct ourselves. They are a wake-up call. They remind us that everyone is somebody's child and grandchild. They remind us of our place in the lineage of the past and the future to come."

When the hour comes to a close, the women very quietly turn to the person on the right, tap her shoulder, and proceed down the sidewalk, leaving as they began, in silence. The traffic continues. The antique shoppers come and go. Several joggers pass.

Each woman will carry the experience into their own lives, knowing that in a small way, they acted to bring change to their immediate surroundings.

Before leaving, Nora says, "When we stand, I imagine the ancestors behind us, and before us, the children of the future."

"Sometimes," says one woman, now shivering from the cold, "what is needed is to stand long enough to mourn, long enough to understand the next person, long enough to take the hand of the next guy without contempt."

In other words, peace in small numbers may bring peace in the world.

WOMEN

Anjana Satpathy

I look at the new salwar suit, which my mother got as a birthday gift. It is a beautiful shade of pale pink similar to the color of an onion peel with a pretty floral embroidered dupatta. I pick up the dupatta impulsively and wrap it around me. Then I drape the dupatta over my head and turn toward the mirror to catch a reflection of myself. It strikes me like a bolt of lightning that I am part of that generation of women who grew up dressing up their Barbies and dreaming about beautiful wedding clothes, but as adults are against most (if not all) gender stereotypes.

I sit down on the bed nearby and think about all the times I had longed for new bangles, bindis, and dupattas and remember my excited baby self putting on oversized bangles belonging to my mom. I remember those times when my mom refused to buy me a Barbie doll in spite of my constant begging. She never liked buying me Barbies or kitchen sets. I did not even know toy kitchen sets existed till I saw it at my cousin's place. That was my mom's way of giving me a gender-neutral upbringing, whatever that means.

And now, when I am an adult and married, I cringe at the thought of having to wear bangles. It is not like I do not love bangles anymore. It is more like my way of saying no to the rule that married Indian women should be wearing bangles at all times, and I am an ordinary girl, not even close to being a social activist.

This is the mindset of most of my contemporaries, friends, and colleagues. We sit and discuss how we won our last small battle. For one of the girls, it can be as small as refusing to wear traditional attire during the last family function. For someone else, it can be as big as fighting for her right to work and be financially independent. There are also times when one just agrees to do something in order to avoid a battle or an unpleasant confrontation. We discuss that too.

The point is not about being a rebel. All of us are ordinary girls looking to find ways to be happy(ier), fighting for our rights, which have been tactfully stolen from us generations ago. We are all ordinary human beings striving to fit into the society, but fighting to retain our own identities. That is definitely an extremely thin line to balance on!

It is not like we do not love the chance to wear a beautiful traditional saree or we do not love our kids. But we still fight against wearing that saree or insist upon going to work in spite of having kids so that this love shall never be able to give others the power to make us powerless, now or in the future. The love for our kids should never stand in the way of being independent women. And the love for wearing sarees should never be expected or prohibit us from wearing something else that we might want to wear.

Our only point is that we, and only we, have the right to make our own choices. No one else should be making them for us.

Women are called the better half, but we are mostly treated as second-class citizens. When we drive a car on the road, there will be people (both men and women) subconsciously thinking that women are bad drivers. Such a level of deep-seated discrimination in people's minds! As a matter of fact, some countries still do not allow women to drive. So, there will be men and women telling us women that we should be happy we are allowed to drive a car. Maybe we should be obliged to the generous men in our community who gave us the right to drive. Sounds hilarious, but that is how it is!

I remember a friend telling me once that she involuntarily feels like the lesser person in front of any man. And this was a perfectly fine, well-educated woman talking! I cringe at the thought of what a less advantaged woman would be feeling or thinking about her status in this male-dominated society. Our social conditioning affects our minds this way. Maybe there should be gender-neutral mental conditioning classes for our minds, similar to strength conditioning classes for our bodies!

This makes me think: were men always *numero uno* and women always came in second? Was it like this since the beginning of evolution? If yes, was there any reasoning behind it? More importantly, if no, why and how did women start believing and accepting we were lesser mortals?

Maybe we will never find out how and why men and women

started behaving the way they behave, when gender inequality sealed and stamped its place in our daily lives. But we can focus on what needs to change.

Things have changed; things have definitely improved from how they were during our mothers' or grandmothers' days. But they need to get better. And it is on our shoulders to ensure that it happens.

Each human being is different in his or her own way. Men and women are different, men and men are different, women and women are different. So, no one can ever be equal or the same in the literal sense. However, we will achieve true equality when everyone—men, women, queer, straight—all have equal rights to choose what they want to do and are free from discrimination in any form. We all have the right to make our own choices and stand by what we feel is right.

We have a long way to reach that goal. In the meantime, we can definitely work on taking small baby steps. Let's do it for the sake of the baby girl who is being gifted a pink dress as you are reading this piece, but might be more inclined toward a navy blue or brown or black.

BLUE, PINK, AND WHITE STRIPES
Aila Alvina Boyd

"What does that pin mean?" one of my students asked me.

The question made my heart feel as though it had dropped down into the depths of my stomach. My breathing grew heavy as I wracked my brain for a viable answer. The truth certainly wouldn't do, I told myself.

"It's… It's…" No matter how hard I tried, I couldn't come up with a lie to cover up the truth about what my lapel pin actually represented.

Finally, the student stood up and walked over to where I was standing. I was perched behind a podium because I had been in the middle of a lecture on Christopher Marlowe, a lesser known but still very important Elizabethan playwright, when the question caught me off guard.

After closely studying the pin for what felt like an eternity, the student said, "It looks like a trans pride flag."

The seconds that followed were incredibly painful. I was in pure agony. I felt as though I had been dropkicked square in the stomach. There was no getting around the fact that she had my number. A veil of silence fell over the usually boisterous class as my Introduction to Theatre students awaited my response.

At that point, I knew I had no other choice than to fess up. I knew that outright lying about what the pin meant would just come across as being a feeble attempt to save my own ass. And besides, we had just finished reading *The Tragedy of Macbeth*, a play that prompted many discussions about honesty and integrity. Despite desperately not wanting to place myself on a vulnerable footing by admitting the symbolism of the pin, I knew that denying that it was a trans pride pin would have been utter hypocritical.

"You're right," I finally admitted, sounding defeated.

Much to my surprise, the students didn't erupt into a boisterous outrage as the result of my candor. Instead, they seemed to mull over the truth about the pin in great detail. I could almost see the little wheels and gears in their heads turning the same way that they did when we discussed ancient Greek playwrights like Aristophanes and Euripides.

Finally, a male student, a football player who had enrolled in my class because he wanted an "easy elective," said, "That's pretty cool." He then nodded his head as though to confirm that there was nothing wrong with me or my pin.

His three simple words broke the awkward silence in the room, giving permission to all of the other students to start engaging in conversations about what it means to be trans. Not wanting to intervene, I slowly made my way over to my desk and eavesdropped on what they were saying. One student talked about how Gigi Gorgeous, a trans woman, is her favorite YouTube personality. Another said that Caitlyn Jenner's speech at the ESPY Awards was the first time he had ever really taken note of a person of trans identity. Her speech, he said, was inspiring. Other positive conversations about trans people took place throughout the other corners of the room. To my great surprise, I didn't hear a single student vocalize any disgust or objection towards the trans community.

The morning that all this occurred was on November 20th, also known as the Transgender Day of Remembrance. I first learned about the occasion when I was a college freshman and was undergoing the first phase of my transition. Although I had never known a trans person who had been murdered, the idea of setting aside one day out of the year to recognize fellow trans people who had been slain because of the simple fact that they dared to live openly as their true gender deeply resonated with me. Having grown up in a rural part of Appalachia, there were times during my youth that I feared physical violence and even death because I didn't conform to other people's ideas of who I should be and what I should look like.

Throughout my college years, my transition progressed to the point that I started to "pass," which came as a great relief. I no longer had to fear that the way I looked would send someone into a verbal or physical rage. Once I reached that point, I didn't want to rock the boat, so I stopped wearing my trans pride pin every November 20th.

It wasn't until I found myself teaching high school in North

Carolina in the midst of the Republican Party's decision to make it illegal for the trans community to use the facilities that correspond to their gender identities that I decided that something had to give. When I woke up on the morning of November 20th, I found myself overwhelmed by a nagging sense of guilt. I was one of the lucky ones. I was able to waltz right into the bathroom of my choice without turning a single head, a luxury that I knew many other trans people didn't possess. The decision to pull out the pin from my bottom drawer and dust it off was a rash one, but I felt certain that something as innocuous as a lapel pin would go unnoticed. I was wrong. And I'm glad that I was.

Ever since that day in class, I make it a point to wear my lapel pin even when the colors clash with my outfits and when I'm sporting something as casual as a T-shirt. Wearing the pin is my, albeit subtle, way of announcing to the world that I'm not ashamed of my trans status. As a result of my decision to start wearing it every day, I've had a lot of frank conversations with my colleagues and even strangers. When asked what the pin stands for, I no longer hedge my response the way that I did that day in class. "It represents trans pride," I proudly declare.

Although it's difficult to know the true feelings that reside in the hearts and minds of the people who have queried about my pin, it should count for something that they have all been kind towards me after I have told them what the blue, pink, and white stripes represent. Many of them have questions about my identity and the trans community as a whole, which is a good thing because change can't occur unless people possess the requisite knowledge.

Little did I know when I fastened it to my blazer that morning that my tiny blue, pink, and white pin would open the door for a conversation that I had been too afraid to broach with my students. As a trans person teaching in a southern state, the state that passed the infamous "Bathroom Bill" no less, I felt as though I had no other option than to tread lightly when I first accepted the position. My students' responses to my pin made me realize that I wasn't as helpless as I thought that I was. It made me realize that I didn't have to barge into class one day and make some grand announcement that I was trans in order to enact change and open people's minds. Giving my students an avenue to talk about what it means to be trans is good enough.

HEALTHCARE JUSTICE

BRENDA'S PLAN

Uzomah Ugwu

I hear Brenda's got a baby
But, Brenda's barely got a brain
A damn shame, the girl can hardly spell her name
(That's not our problem, that's up to Brenda's family)
Well let me show ya how it affects the whole community
    -Tupac from "Brenda's Got a Baby"

Got the cover-ups that tuck
in forgotten to be mothers up
In beds set like traps to shut up the public
Ripped in parts the right to decide
is so hard to pick up their
Civil liberalities, marching on the dimes

Earned from their thriving Times
in office that has made
Them their billions where
they can build their own bel air
When to everyone else it is better off
Pulling a dog day afternoon to feed your family

Medically dispositioned and pressed
against a wall of hypocrisy and laws
Where we all fall as unknown soldiers
of democracy just known by Phis'
Combine with conflict driven paths
to make us feel the sense of what it means to die
Over and over again in addition to the nonsense
of the madness that economically never ends

Insufficient funds and lump-sided agendas
to keep us the beggars
Lets the baby in Brenda's belly
know it is better in a dumpster
Then with a parenthood planned
By any government when it will have
to face such a bleak future

And how could she know how to nurture another life
When never having one as a child denied by the
Same political channels that separated her family
And keeps tearing families apart
While they place more
one-sided deals on the table

With our social security, safe in their bonds
and hedge funds
To be traded where in the end
it leaves us out of the equation

Just a pawn in their Money games
and they are holding the profits
Not a real player, so as we carve out the edge
Of our existence trying to witness only
Leaves tears dried up on the victims of this system,
Just waiting for more merciless actions
Yet I am numb to it all unaffected by the treason
With no reason but to get that money ball
No need for it to be the right season
For sessions are held in halls, not regarding the
Interest of the Townspeople that form this nation at all
Across a beaten street a kid screaming and running

As if someone was pulling their teeth
trying to escape and get
Past the reaper of their innocence
That makes it so no one has freedom at last
Or had it to begin with,

Maybe that is why with the stress
Brenda loses her child
Before she decided to let it
live or end its life before it began.
Better off than being told what to do with it
She holds her empty belly from time to time
Wondering if God is on her side.

I HAVE NOT FORGOTTEN
HOW TO FIGHT

Carole Ann Moleti

I was born to be an Italian-American princess: dripping gold chains, hair teased as high as my heels, wearing pushups and plunging necklines, and being indulged by my parents and hand-picked husband.

For the first 18 years of my life, I didn't know that any other religion existed besides Roman Catholicism. During twelve years of Catholic school, the Sisters of the Divine Compassion punished violations of the Ten Commandments by banging heads against blackboards and swats with rulers and rosary beads. Not eating meat on Friday was the eleventh, and when that was rescinded it indicated to me there was room for interpretation with the others, too. I learned a lot of prayers, most of which I have forgotten.

As a pampered, protected youngster, I loved the magical electrical flashes that blazed like bolts of lightning through the windows in our third-floor walk-up when the wheels of the Number 6 Pelham Bay Local ran over the third rail. There was a courtyard outside, but no grass, trees, or other reminder that the Bronx had once been a rural escape from the tenements of lower Manhattan.

Throughout the borough, development wiped out whole neighborhoods, destroying homes to make room for huge housing projects, roads, and bridges. Carved up portions remained, shadowed by elevated roadways, despoiled by traffic and fumes. The "nice" people moved to Westchester, and those who had nowhere else to go moved in. When the rent didn't get paid and the buildings became run down, landlords torched them for the insurance money, and took off leaving blackened hulks and empty lots where there had once been thriving communities.[1]

My family escaped to a waterfront enclave in the far reaches of the Northeast Bronx. My parents tried to "protect" my two sisters and me, sending us to private schools, and we hunkered down in our pastoral enclave.

I vividly remember asking my sobbing mother why the black horse at President John F. Kennedy's funeral had boots backwards in the stirrups. Dr. Martin Luther King, Jr. was assassinated the night before my Confirmation. When Robert F. Kennedy was killed, I wondered why being in favor of equal rights for all was cause for death.

Prejudice and out-front racism was a way of life. I heard tales of "spics" and "niggers" moving in. They spoke Spanglish and street English, dressed differently, and had different customs.

Immolated by arson, the Bronx became a study in the effects of urban development and poverty. Live, on color television, a fire blazed as a helicopter hovered over a game at Yankee Stadium, showcasing to the nation the demise of the Grand Concourse, once the home of wealthy lawyers and judges who wanted to live near the county courthouse.

My father became an environmental activist to call attention to the pollution of the East River by businesses as well as private citizens dumping waste in estuaries leading to it. The Ferry Point and Pelham Bay Landfills were subsequently remediated as superfund sites. They smelled so bad on summer nights we couldn't keep our windows open.

He lobbied as a member of Community Board #10, and I went along with him for meetings and occasional protests. He once spray-painted cars wrecked in accidents that were dumped on the street by the Triboro Bridge and Tunnel Authority.

As a young teen, I researched and gave presentations to community organizations on the hazards of dumping garbage into the oceans.

I recall the televised images of students at Kent State University lying dead on the ground. On his way home from work, my father was caught up in a bottle and brick throwing incident with hardhats who attacked anti-war protestors on the campus of Columbia University.[2]

I went from being pampered and protected into the heart of a very dangerous New York City. At a public university in the era of free tuition, a big Black dude sold marijuana as a daily special in the cafeteria. At the height of the fiscal crisis, free tuition was ended and there were building takeovers and sit-ins.

In biology class, my professor told dirty jokes as part of his lessons. I took English classes with professors who had us reading books that confronted controversial topics like abortion, and religious preaching wasn't part of the discussions. Straight A's did not get me into closed-out classes, but flirting with male department chairpersons worked every time.

The guy who wandered around, flapping his hands, muttering to himself, and randomly coming up to women and staring directly into their faces, reeked of body odor and trouble. He once chased me through a labyrinthine tunnel under the buildings when I walked alone one cold, rainy day. I escaped like a pack of mongrels was after me, despite a backpack full of textbooks.

Women my age had had abortions and weren't embarrassed or contrite. And gays and lesbians celebrated their lifestyle. My world was no longer black and white, right and wrong, Italian or Irish, Catholic or Jewish. There were rainbows, and gray areas when the moral/ethical debates threw shadows, a melting pot, and more gods to worship than I ever imagined possible.

I worked with fellow nursing students who were starting a campus nursing health and information center. We met with an executive from Blue Cross and Blue Shield who told us "he" would not pay for abortions because of "a fling in the backseat of a car." I wrote him a letter afterwards reminding him that there were both male and female "flingers" involved in conceptions. He sent a letter of apology for his insensitivity. Blue Cross did offer the first policies for college students. That center is still open, forty years after I graduated.

◻◻◻

New York City was in bankruptcy in the 1970s. Life felt like a scene out of *Batman*: racial tension, vigilantes, murders, and arson. When the big blackout of 1977 hit, the glass started breaking, looters took to the streets, and I barely got to my car in time. I battled my way home, gas gauge on empty, with no traffic lights, prepared to run over anyone who swung at my windshield with a baseball bat.

Curtis and Lisa Sliwa's *Guardian Angels* and Bernie Goetz going ballistic on a subway car and taking out a couple of muggers bookended Son of Sam. He prowled lovers' lanes for brown-eyed brunettes parked with their boyfriends. When he blew Donna Lauria's brains out in my neighborhood, this abdicated princess with long brown hair and a high school sweetheart had a bull's eye on her forehead.

Snipers took pot shots at emergency medical teams and firefighters, who nicknamed their firehouses "Fort Apache" and "Little House on the Prairie." I was confronted by a mob of Black teenagers on my way to classes one day, but had learned in psych how to de-escalate — and it worked.

I walked the streets and saw the desperation caused by poverty, racism, and urban blight. And learned that nothing good comes without a struggle, no matter how well behaved you are and how much you pray. Sister Mary Assumpta, who once controlled a class of fifty-two children, did teach me something useful: Never flinch or you're done for.

ᗒᗒᗒ

I survived, and graduated, ready to take on the world. Devouring *The Hite Report* by Shere Hite, and *Our Bodies, Ourselves* by the Boston Women's Health Collective at the age of twenty-one was like discovering the liberation of tampons when I was fourteen. I decided that I wanted to work with women so that no one had to wait as long as I had to find that out.

Progressing through a logical sequence of job titles and levels of responsibility, I descended toward hell and onto the mean streets of the South Bronx, Harlem, and Washington Heights. I threw food into rubble-strewn lots to feed starving dogs and cats. This Whitey was crazy enough to stick it out through the crack cocaine epidemic of the 1980s that made heroin addicts look like kindly old souls.

I was inspired by my nursing professors and the stories of other women who used their social status to further the health and well-being of the poor, particularly women and children.

In an era when women were second-class citizens, their work meaningless, and their brains "too feeble to think and act without the supervision of a man," Florence Nightingale published *Notes on Nursing: What It Is and What It Is Not* in 1859. It is still cited today.

In 1908, Lavinia Dock recognized the dynamics of sexism, and was politically active, using both traditional and subversive forces to create social change.[3] Dock revered Nightingale as a pioneer in insisting that nursing was a profession in its own right, based on an intimate relationship with patients which was not subject to control by physicians.

Dock spent her life working for social justice: to expose the conditions in sweatshops, to tear apart the Nurses' Associated Alumnae (which became the American Nurses' Association) when they rejected a woman's suffrage resolution. She asserted that war contributed to the re-emergence and persistence of disease.[4] Upon her death, the president of the American Nurses' Association eulogized Miss Dock as "sometimes too forthright to be tactful." Because of her somewhat "puckish sense of humor, the validity of her purposes were not always understood and appreciated."[5]

My great-grandmother was a public health nurse like me. A lay midwife doing home births, licensed in 1911, she had thirteen children, only eight of whom survived. She cared for immigrant women in the same area of the Bronx I now work in. I did not know that until I'd chosen nurse-midwifery as my specialty. I was born the year after Lavinia Dock died. I imagine they knew each other. Whether odd coincidence or destiny, I have often been told, like Miss Dock, that my direct approach, colorful language, and sense of humor are not appreciated.

To that I say, "March on, sisters!"

◻◻◻

Being a woman in a woman's profession taking care of women was a triple handicap. I graduated at the top of my class, but it didn't mean much, making less than sanitation workers even though I was responsible for the lives of mothers and their babies.

I cared for patients having abortions, many undergoing second trimester procedures for genetic disorders. Most delivered at night when I was working alone. Maybe it was the darkness, or anguished whispers in the night as I injected pain medication by a flashlight balanced on the bedside table that made it surreal.

A battle-hardened head nurse had explained that in the days before legal abortion, women died from trying to self-induce abortions with coat hangers and other sharp objects, or by injecting green soap or other chemicals into their vaginas with turkey basters. Some went to unlicensed practitioners. The women would arrive in the emergency room hemorrhaging, or with raging infections, or with their uteri perforated and damaged by incorrect techniques.

After being promoted to assistant head nurse of the labor and delivery suite, I snuck into the delivery rooms and dumped the leather and metal shoulder restraints that some doctors insisted we put on women in labor to keep them from moving around too much. I buried them under bags of bloody garbage. The mystery is now solved.

◻◻◻

I have walked the streets in some of the worst neighborhoods in New York City during the worst times, when there were more abandoned buildings than inhabited ones, and more starving dogs and stray cats than people.

I am more terrified now. I care for immigrants, many of them from the Middle East, Africa, and Central America, who are emaciated, malnourished, fearful victims of violence and abuse, now having panic attacks and PTSD flashbacks.

I would really rather be going about my business, secure in the knowledge that the country is in the hands of a sane, competent president and Congress whose only agenda is safeguarding the health, well-being, and safety of all citizens of the United States, regardless of their political party, gender, sexual orientation, race, or ethnicity.

And an executive branch that honors treaties with other nations, and sees that the United States extends a helping hand to those who need it because of war, natural disasters, or terrorism. And elected officials who don't lie, cheat, steal, shake down, intimidate, rape and assault women, and evade paying taxes.

And an administration that is intelligent enough to believe the science of climate change is real, and that without decisive action the Earth will not survive the continued onslaught of misuse, abuse, and overuse by greedy nations and corporations who damage, pollute, contaminate, and destroy our resources in the name of jobs and profits for the 1-percent.

I won't betray the trust of anyone who has told me about the abortions they, their sisters, their mothers, their aunt, girlfriends or wives had, but still insist they're 'pro-life.' But because of hypocrites that 'choose life,' those who face that agonizing choice will find it harder or someday maybe impossible to choose when they will have a child, and they may die.

I'm sick of women's healthcare being threatened by dirty old men who refuse to take responsibility for their actions. And are becoming senators, congressmen, and Supreme Court justices despite what they have done.

Like most of my friends and colleagues, I value honesty, integrity, truth, and providing the greatest good for the greatest number. I believe everyone should have safe housing, clean water, nutritious food, and medical care. I believe all are equal no matter what their income, religion, country of origin, race, or gender identity.

I'm tired of becoming physically ill listening to racist rhetoric, climate deniers, gun freaks who don't care that people, including children, are dying in mass shootings, violent storms wiping out entire islands, and hate crimes — not only because of inaction — but also because the deviant behavior of mentally ill persons is being reinforced and is spreading like plague.

I'm still a Bronx girl, and I love being on the streets, mixing it up in the melting pot. I wear one gold chain my mother brought me from Florence, Italy but the crucifix is somewhere in my jewelry box. I don't go to church much, but when I do, I pray the Our Father, the Hail Mary, and the Glory Be that this ongoing nightmare in the United States will soon end.

I always play it and say it straight. I march. I protest. I write letters. I make phone calls. I resist, and like Elizabeth Warren, I persist.

I am not going back. And I have not forgotten how to fight.

Sources

[1]Jonnes, Jill. *We're Still Here: The Rise, Fall and Resurrection of the South Bronx*. New York. Atlantic Monthly Press, 1986.

[2] Cowie, Jefferson. "The 'Hard Hat Riot' was a Preview of Today's Political Divisions." *The New York Times*, May 11, 2020, https://www.nytimes.com/2020/05/11/nyregion/hard-hat-riot.html?smid=em-share. Accessed 16 May 2020.

[3] Chinn, Peggy L. "Historical Roots: Female Nurses and Political Action." *Journal of the New York State Nurses' Association*, vol. 16, no. 2, 1985, pp. 29-34.

[4] Chinn, op. cit.

[5] Roberts, Mary. "Editorials: Lavinia Lloyd Dock." *American Journal of Nursing*, vol. 56, 1956, p.727.

SILENCES: ROE VS. WADE

Patti Capel Swartz

In the summer of 1966, when I realized beyond a doubt that I was pregnant, I had a love affair with a telephone pole. Going home from university summer classes each day as I headed into a very sharp curve on my route, I debated whether or not this was the day. I was afraid of what my dad would do if he learned I was pregnant, and what my parents' friends would think, because girls just were not supposed to have babies without being married then. One of my distant cousins had gotten pregnant. The guy refused to marry her, and my mother made sure I knew how the neighbors acted toward her and what it would mean to that child to be what she called a bastard.

"Poor baby," Mother said. "Punished for something that wasn't his fault. She would have married the guy, but he said it wasn't his problem. Take a lesson from what poor Ruthie is going through. Don't get yourself in that fix."

Adding to my fear and depression, I couldn't believe the stories that my friend Jenny told us when we used to sit on the floor in the hallway of our dorm during my second year of college, very early morning hours talking and eating frozen orange juice concentrate liberated from the dining hall freezer. I had a hard time believing her until she showed us the scars from the hangers with which her dad had beaten her. She never wanted to go home for visits. And then she got pregnant. She knew her dad would beat her if he found out, so she went to a back-alley abortionist. This was the early 1960s when abortion wasn't legal, but beating your children was. Too many women had to go to an abortionist whose care was less than stellar, where the risk of infection and uncontrolled bleeding was very real. At the time, we thought Jenny would be all right, but things went wrong. She had to be admitted to the hospital to stop her hemorrhaging. Then her dad did find out. We never saw her again.

In the 1960s, when I was young, there was no birth control, and "nice" girls like Jenny and me didn't know how to keep from getting pregnant or how to miscarry, nor did we know who to ask. Not our mothers. They would be scandalized. Not our usual doctors. They might report to our parents. We were truly alone in a world where this situation was not mentioned except in terms of censure.

Afraid to go where Jenny had gone, I talked to another friend who had been pregnant twice. She told me, "You've gotta have an abortion! You know, the first time, my mother took me on a cruise to Puerto Rico so that no one would know. It was beautiful there, but so awful because she made me give the baby up. I was pregnant all that time, and then I had to give the baby up. It was horrible. The second time I knew I couldn't go through that again, so I had the abortion. I went to a really good doctor. He's expensive, but he's a good doctor, not one of those back-alley butchers that sliced Jenny up so badly." She gave me a telephone number.

It took me several days to work up my courage to call from a phone booth at the Piggly-Wiggly Supermarket parking lot on my way home from classes. Even though the day was hot and the sun reflecting off the silver metal of the booth, I was shaking. The call was answered by a woman. When I said I would like to talk to Mr. Lane, as I had been told to do, the woman said, "Mr. Lane is never in. Can I take some information?" She asked me how far along I was. Because my periods were very irregular, I wasn't sure. I think I said six weeks, but I was probably further along than that. I never got a call back. The clinic was closed down, I guess. That happened quite a lot. This doctor, an M.D. who believed that young women's lives should not be ruined by a pregnancy nor should they die from a botched abortion, was arrested several times, and, I believe, even served jail time for practicing what he believed: that young women should have the right to control their own bodies.

When I got no call back, I didn't know what to do. I was graduating from college in August. I had my life planned out. A stint at a resident company, then grad school and teaching and directing plays in college. I had already auditioned at a resident company and I had gotten a call that I had received a fellowship. Not knowing what else to do and hoping for a miracle, I went there having told the director of the company nothing.

In acting classes in late October, the instructor for the class asked to speak to me. "Are you pregnant?" he asked, "Or are you eating way too many vegetables?' He encouraged me to speak to the playhouse director who let me stay. Then I went home to explain to my mother that I would not be home for the holidays. After I told her, she said, "It sounds like you have your mind made up." That was all she said.

I worked with a placement agency. I can never forget the extreme depression of that time, parking on the street next to a very old cemetery in the heart of the city, pushing through the icy wind off the lake, trying to make plans. When my water broke, a friend drove me to the hospital and called my mother after the baby was born. She came to my room, puzzled. She said the only question my mother asked was, "Is Pat all right?" Then thanked her for calling. My friend said she could not believe that my mother didn't want to know about the baby.

I never saw my baby. I thought if I did, I could never give him up. Each of the several days I was in the hospital, I walked almost to the viewing window of the nursery, but I was too upset to actually look so I turned back at the edge of the window, something I still regret. I have carried this sadness and self-loathing because of my cowardice with me all of my adult life.

At that time, everyone told an unmarried mother that adoption was what she should do. I thought I had to give my baby up, so I did, so that he could have a better life. Then I wanted more than anything else to have another baby. I found out later when I worked as a caseworker in adoptions that often happens. When you give up a baby, you have a desire to replace him or her. But I didn't know that then.

Still I didn't intend to get married. Seeing my sisters' bad marriages was enough of that for me. But the deep sadness in my life made me change my plans. I married a man I had met that fall. He took care of me emotionally and physically throughout the pregnancy and I felt I owed him for that. But marrying him was the worst mistake of my life.

After a year or two when we thought we were financially stable enough, I tried to "get pregnant," but it didn't work. He was tested first. I remember my gynecologist telling me that I didn't have "a Chinaman's chance in hell" to get pregnant with him and that if I wanted to have children that it would have to be with someone else. He asked if I wanted to tell him, or should he. He showed so much "compassion" I felt I had no choice. I said I would, and I did, saying that both of us had problems. He believed me. Or so he said. He had been a fairly heavy drinker for as long as I had known him, but after that his drinking increased. He banked on my guilt and used it to keep me in the marriage.

Because we both wanted children we applied for adoption. There was pressure from my mother, too. "What would a life without children be?" she said. We went through the horribly invasive process of a home study. My husband's drinking continued. Finally, just as I was almost determined to leave him because of his alcoholism, I needed two surgeries within three months, and I needed to stay. Only about three months after this, while I was still recovering, we were notified by an adoption agency that they were placing an infant with us. After the baby was placed, things got better. I was happier, even though I thought about my other baby every day, and my husband drank less. Eventually two more children were placed with us.

I loved my children. They were my children even though I had not given birth to them. I couldn't have loved them more if I had birthed them. I stayed in the marriage for a long time, for the kids. Not only did I think they needed a stable life with two parents, but I had no way of supporting them. On "Black Monday" in the early 1970s the steel industry in our area shut down suddenly leaving financial chaos in its wake. The economy was horrific. If I left my marriage, I had three children without the means to support them and no prospects of finding work. As the economy worsened, so did my husband's drinking. Finally, I couldn't stand it anymore.

After an uncle died, I used the money he left me to go back to college to earn credentials to teach. In lieu of a teaching position when one was not forthcoming, I worked as an adoption recruiter and I was finally able to move out of the house. After eighteen years of marriage and a four-year fight over the children, property, and all of the divisions that come with breaking up a marriage, we were divorced.

The only good thing the divorce accomplished was that during that time and until he died my ex-husband began going to AA and stopped drinking. He was, however, a dry drunk, and his abusive behavior to all of us didn't change all that much. This divorce was emotionally devastating for all of us. None of us ever fully recovered.

I carried that extra burden of placing a child. I know what having a baby and giving that baby up because I had no choice about what abortion did to my life. It also had horrific consequences for my children. Because of the problems we faced due to my actions and those of my ex-husband, and because I had had no right to choose, I began volunteering at a women's center as an escort. At that time clinic doctors and staff were being murdered, clinics bombed, and many people died for asserting a woman's right to choose, to control this aspect of her life. All of this violence in the name of "right to life." As an escort, I helped women who came for counseling or a procedure to get inside without being as harassed as they would have been otherwise by anti-abortion pickets who believed then and still believe it is their God-given right to tell every woman what to do with her own body.

One Saturday, I got a call about a possible attack on the local clinic. My daughter was a teenager and she was at home, but I volunteered to come into the clinic. I dropped my daughter at a friend's house and went to sit inside the clinic. There were no procedures that day. There were no appointments. We thought if there were people inside it was less likely that the clinic would be destroyed. There were about ten of us inside, men and women, sitting there all day from nine in the morning to five in the afternoon, trying to be brave, telling stories. The doors were locked, but also two-by-fours were braced against them. This was prevention against the demonstrators getting in, but I realized if the clinic was bombed it might have prevented us getting out. The front section of the building was glass, and it would have been easy to shatter the door or the windows. It was one of the longest days I have ever spent. I kept thinking, what if I get killed? What will happen to my daughter? But I had to do it, to volunteer and to stay there all day because I didn't want what happened to me and, consequently, my children, to happen to someone else. It's just not right for anyone else to make a decision about someone's body and someone's life. I had to be there. It was the right thing for me to do.

Since that day, after I earned first a master's degree and then a PhD., it has been the right thing for me to teach gender studies classes and composition classes to help students understand the very real need of a woman's right to choose. While this is a small contribution, teaching about women's rights and the right to choose is at least something. Perhaps this is a way of paying forward because of my own experiences or perhaps it is a payment of a debt because of the circumstances of my own life. I only hope that it has helped other women to make whatever choice is right for them.

MAKING STRIDES WITH EVERY STEP

Lisa Braxton

The Charles River Esplanade, a green and flowering oasis in the heart of Boston, is a popular place for cyclists, picnickers, parents pushing strollers, and college kids looking to rent kayaks and sailboats. However, when I was there on a Sunday in September, the majority of park visitors had a different activity in mind: completing a five-mile fundraising walk—while wearing lots of pink. Men strolled confidently on the esplanade wearing pink tutus over their jeans. A group of women donned shocking pink troll wigs that resembled giant cones of cotton candy. Some walkers were ebullient as they punched at the sky with their pink pom poms. Others playfully flung carnation pink feather boas over their shoulders. Pink tiaras full of bling were a common sight.

I couldn't have felt more at home.

That morning as I dressed for the Making Strides Against Breast Cancer walk, I glanced ever so often at the email I'd received earlier in the week from the American Cancer Society, trying to work up my nerve to follow its directive: "Don't hold back on your pink attire," it read. "The crazier you look, the better."

Normally one to dress conservatively in darker shades, I forced myself out of my comfort zone. I left home wearing a salmon pink knit top, fuchsia crop pants, a hot pink fanny pack and neon pink high-topped sneakers. I would have accented the ensemble with pale pink sweat socks if I could have found some.

As I completed the first mile with some sorority sisters and the other 25,000 participants, I reflected on how odd it was for me to be participating in a fundraising walk at all. On a fairly regular basis on Sunday mornings, I was one of those drivers being held up at an intersection by a traffic cop while runners or walkers for some cause or another crossed in front of me. I'd be annoyed, thinking that they were responsible for my being late for the praise and worship portion of church service. I'd wish that they would move a little faster or take another route next time. Now I was one of them who annoyed other drivers.

Four months before the walk, I was lying face down in an MRI machine for a combination breast MRI/biopsy procedure, my face wet with tears. I was told by the nurses and technicians to try to lie on the table as motionless as possible for the several hours I would be there and was given a panic button to press in case I got claustrophobic in the narrow tube. Earplugs were squeezed into my ears to soften the knocking and buzzing noises of the magnets.

I'd been through an emotionally grueling several months of repeat mammograms, and ultrasounds. One doctor had stated that my dense breast tissue on one side had her concerned. It was so dense that if something was wrong with me, she wouldn't be able to see it. Another doctor noted that the breast tissue on the right looked different than the tissue on the left, which didn't necessarily mean that something was wrong, but she couldn't be sure. An initial MRI was ordered. Two days later, when my primary care doctor called me, I knew something was wrong. Not only were there spots on the right side in the location of the dense breast tissue that had raised concern, she said, but spots were also identified on the left. She said the next recommended step would be the combination breast MRI/biopsy.

As I lay in the tube of the machine, my thumb gently caressing the panic button, I prayed. I prayed as hard as I could that it was a false alarm, that I didn't have breast cancer and that my life could return to normal.

A few hours later once the procedures were done, the surgeon who'd performed the biopsy met with me in an exam room. "I don't like to give my patients false hope while they're waiting for the pathology report to come in," she said, her voice gentle and soothing. "I'm pretty sure it's cancer."

I was numb. I asked her whether or not I would have to have a mastectomy, chemo, and/or radiation, but I felt as if I was outside of my body, watching myself ask her those questions. She responded that the cancer was very small, which meant that my treatment could be minimally invasive. But the specialists would be the ones to discuss next steps with me.

My life moved in fast forward after the pathology report confirmed my diagnosis. Appointments were scheduled with the surgeon, radiation oncologist, and medical oncologist. My cancer was Stage 1. I was offered the choice of a lumpectomy with the cancerous tissue and tissue removed around the cancer to create clean margins. The breast would remain intact. Chemo would not be necessary. I entered a clinical trial which concluded that my risk of recurrence would be the same whether I had radiation or not. I was prescribed an oral medication in pill form that I would have to take for five years to block the agents that created the kind of environment in which cancer cells could grow. Remarkably, within a week of my surgery, I was back at work.

I felt a range of emotions during this period of time, deep sadness and grief, despair and sometimes moments of joy because of the family and friends who surrounded me with their love and comfort. I was heartbroken that I had breast cancer, but relieved that it was caught early. Relieved that women are encouraged to have annual mammograms. And relieved that we have the highly advanced technology of MRI machines that can see what a mammogram can't. I thought about the activists who have gone to Congress over the years to push for funding for breast cancer research, the doctors who specialize in breast care and are vigilant about identifying cancer and treating it, all of the people on a grassroots level who do their part to raise awareness about the importance of breast cancer research, early detection, and breast care. I thought about the fundraising car washes, tea parties, hair cutting marathons, raffles, and walkathons. I wanted to thank them all. I thought the best way for me to do that was to take action.

On social media, I happened to come across a post from a friend who was conducting an online fundraiser for Making Strides Against Breast Cancer and stated that she would be participating in the walk. I went to the Making Strides website and followed the directions for setting up my own online fundraiser. In my post I also vowed to participate in the walk. I raised about $100 and thanked all of those who contributed.

A few days later, I got an invitation in the mail for a Making Strides kickoff event, a pep rally of sorts in downtown Boston, to generate enthusiasm for the upcoming walk. I decided to attend the kickoff. I was handed a sash to wear with the word "Survivor" emblazoned in pink and met other survivors who proudly wore their sashes. A professional photographer hired for the event took pictures, including one of me holding a pink pinwheel next to a basket of pinwheels to be planted in a "Garden of Hope" on the esplanade during the walk.

Days after the kickoff, I got a call from one of the Making Strides coordinators. They wanted to use my photo on the website to encourage the public to participate in the walk and make pledges of donations. I told them I would be happy to help. Later, a few friends let me know that they had received emails from the American Cancer Society about the walk and were surprised to see my photo as part of the plea.

As I ticked off one mile after the other during the five-mile walk, I not only raised dollars for the cause but chatted with one of the coordinators of Faces of Faith, an annual photographic exhibit of cancer survivors focused on sharing stories of survivorship to encourage the demystification of cancer. The exhibit also supports those who are living witnesses that one can maintain a vibrant life as a cancer survivor. During the program a new set of portraits of cancer survivors will be unveiled. I agreed to be one of the breast cancer survivors giving remarks about my journey.

It took a medical diagnosis to get me from annoyed driver to walk-a-thon participant. I'm feeling pretty comfortable in my high-topped neon-pink sneakers and survivors sash. Something tells me that other opportunities won't be far off.

AT THE PAIN CLINIC

Terry Sanville

My wife has more things wrong with her back than the Trump Administration has ethics problems. Her neurologist just shook her head when she spoke of bone spurs, spinal stenosis, scoliosis, herniated disks (yes, plural!), and sciatica. Her primary care physician had a similar response but at least, on request, referred her to a pain clinic for evaluation and treatment.

We're thankful for having access to Medicare and that system has more than once saved our ageing keisters from financial disaster. But even with federal help and gap insurance, our medical expenses last year took more than 30% of our pension incomes. And now my wife is faced with another series of chronic conditions that produce copious amounts of pain, but might not be fixable.

We arrived at the pain clinic a half hour before her appointed time. It's located along a highway with lots of traffic roaring past. The clinic's parking lot was full, with people double parked in the handicapped zone. I dropped my wife off along with her walker and circled the block, finally finding a vacant space. I had no idea that pain is so prevalent.

The clinic's building is a two-story affair with offices and patient treatment on the second floor. The cramped elevator might hold two people in wheelchairs or walkers. It's in constant use since most people in pain can't climb stairs. Coming out of the elevator I was shocked to find patients standing and sitting along the breezeway that led to the clinic offices. Inside the cramped waiting room, patients filled the few chairs, many with heads bent, scratching on the thirteen pages of paperwork that first-timers must fill out. Try doing that in your lap without a clipboard.

More people piled into the office. I left my wife to her clerical duties and stood outside in the breezeway, on a pop-out balcony exposed to the raucous din of highway traffic and the cold morning wind. More patients exited the elevator. The place reminded me of an old college stunt of seeing how many students could be crammed into a Volkswagen Bug.

As I stood elbow-to-elbow with patients and their spouses, it was easy to tell that most of us were geezers, many in walkers or wheelchairs, some with canes. They looked resigned to their internal battle with pain. The few younger adults and small children seemed out of place. I was glad for their presence since the kids were the only ones smiling. It's probably too much to expect smiling faces at a pain clinic. But I did feel an overwhelming sense of empathy and kindness from the group as each made room for the new arrivals. I studied the lined and wrinkled masks, the slumped or standing bodies quietly waiting for their name to be called. I could almost feel that craving for sweet relief that allows clenched jaws to relax, for smiles and maybe even uninterrupted sleep to return.

I stood next to a gray-bearded fellow with an impressive belly covered by a bright print shirt. He recounted how his feet had been mangled while fighting as a Marine in Vietnam. Yet there he *stood* next to me in the cold wind. He claimed to have so much metal in him that he never could make it through airport security without being thoroughly *'wanded.'* A retired college professor with multiple degrees, he taught physics and math at prestigious universities, and loved to ramble on about science.

"After 42 years, I can't stop," he said, grinning.

"Robert!" a voice called and off he trundled for a urine test, and then a brief visit with a doctor and their physician assistant.

He'd stood there for thirty minutes, teaching me about the physics of the universe, not complaining about pain or his disabilities, a patient patient, and a true Marine.

My father was also a Marine and a stoic. Like the Spartans, I think our culture values stoics, people who internalize their problems and don't bother the rest of us with their issues. But in my father's case, being a stoic probably killed him. One night, he complained about chest pains, but wouldn't go to the hospital, claiming it was likely heartburn that would go away. By the next morning, the pain was intolerable, with major parts of his heart muscle destroyed by the attack. If he would have sought treatment immediately....

My father's death taught me not to wait. I stared at the pain clinic's patients and wondered how many of them suffered in silence before showing up to crowd into that airy breezeway. Do we look down on people who complain about pain? Do we expect people to just suck it up? And what is the payoff for the persons who maintain their stoicism?

My wife joined me on the breezeway and we waited. A woman leaned toward a man next to her and murmured, "There's only two doctors, you know — and just look at all of us."

By then I had become numb to my surroundings. Finally, they called my wife's name. The doctor was the picture of efficiency. He prescribed injections for some parts of her back pain, new meds for nerve pain, low dosage opioids for when the pain became intolerable, and arranged for a consult with a spinal surgeon to address the most serious stenosis problem. The doctor spoke in direct terms, outlining the consequences of not pursuing treatment — all in a serious, intense, ten-minute consultation while his assistant furiously keyed chart notes into their computer system.

Our morning at the pain clinic made me wonder about the federal government's war on opiate abuse and how many of the abusers began by using the drugs for legitimate reasons — to treat pain. It scares me that at some moment, my wife or I might be refused medications over concern for drug abuse and addiction. I would humbly suggest that the Feds focus *more* on fostering the development of non-addictive pain medications and new treatments, especially those that deal with *chronic* problems. It should not be a crime to want pain to go away.

NATURAL NEIGHBORHOOD

Keith A. Raymond

The day Aurélie died, the entire community of Auvers-sur-Oise mourned. She was a beautiful seven-year-old girl more often seen running with flowers than skipping rope in the square. Her parents claimed it was the pills she took the day she died. The courts and the pharmaceutical company disagreed. Their attorney whispered in Pierre's ear 'it was an inactive ingredient in the pill' as he stuffed a wad of cash in his pocket outside the courthouse after the case was dismissed. Then he walked away.

The alderman would have none of it. Something had to be done. In protest, the fine folks of Auvers-sur-Oise gave up all their pharmaceuticals. Closed the apothecary and drove the pharmacist from the village. Still, they needed an alternative for their diabetics, their injured, their epileptics, and all the rest.

As they did back in the Middle Ages, the villagers turned to their herbalist. Yvette was tending her garden when a small crowd gathered before her maisonette. Holding a trowel in her delicate hand, she blew a wisp of golden hair from her forehead. As one, they lifted their hands, palms to the heavens. Yvette smiled, her time had come.

Glancing around, she handed Genevieve foxglove for her husband's heart. For the Verlaine's pain, a bouquet of bleeding poppies. For Étienne, a handful of slippery elm for his throat. For pregnant Delphine, she collected raspberries, and also handed her their leaves for tea. Finally, for Alderman Lucien, Yvette dug into her apron pocket and handed him fenugreek seeds. She told him that Jacques's sow could provide him with insulin.

Things returned to the pastoral peace the folks of Auvers-sur-Oise had known. Soon Pierre and Evangeline were the only ones that carried the burden of their grief. Yvette wandered by their house after market to see the curtains drawn. She tinkled the doorbell that once mirrored their happiness.

Evangeline willed herself up from her chair and answered the door in frightful hair. "Yvette, bonjour, ça va?"

"Mon Dieu, Evangeline, Aurélie would not want to see you so sad. Come dear, I've brought you something. Something to lighten your load."

"Go away, witch. Leave us in mourning."

"But Madame, it has been too long. Here, take this. It's for you and Pierre. The flowers for your belly, and the leaves for your sadness," handing her a bouquet of St. John's Wort.

"Leave them at the door. Maybe Pierre will bring them in. They are too yellow for my sad eyes."

Yvette carried her baguette and the rest of her groceries home, whistling. She saw Evangeline out of the corner of her eye, sneaking a hand out to grab the bouquet.

A month later, Spring lit up the town. The people were aglow. The Pharma attorney, while passing through, stopped for fresh cherries, amazed by the radiance of the villagers.

"Where's your pharmacy?" he asked, thinking about a refill he needed.

"We've all been healthier, since he left. Never better. Best thing to happen when he Van Gogh," said Lucien, seeing their nemesis.

The attorney, perhaps mishearing, turned, and the village went impressionistic. Yvette emerged from the painting, waving to him in enchantment.

ENVIRONMENTAL JUSTICE

EARTH IS GOD

Naida Mujkic

It's been 15 days since I came
To the land of Aborigines, at the end of the world,
but I still haven't seen any Aborigine
At souvenir shops smiling Chinese women are selling
Aboriginal items, bracelets, colourful bowls and
embroidered purses, some dead plants and kangaroo
landscapes
Saying that right that item which caught
My eye, right that one, is a true Aboriginal symbol
Leave me alone, woman, my head is full of symbolism
But I'm not telling her that
Instead, I'm asking her: "Where are the Aborigines?"
"They aren't here, they're up in the mountains," says
the shop assistant
So I went up to the mountains, the blue mountains
And I saw snow on mimosas and magnolia trees
Looking like a veil, and confused fern
And wild cockatoo birds
Waddling on one leg like comedians
And a tiny tea house at the edge of the road
Serving English tea
Fuck, I don't want tea, where are the Aborigines?
"They aren't here. They're in the desert," said the
foresters
So I went to the desert
With my eyes covered with a piece of bed sheet, other
parts
I might need
When I told my mother where I was
She thought I was joking
"You're not right in your head," she told me, and I

confirmed, but nothing could be done now
I'm lighting a cigarette in despair, the sun is scorching
Like Your Word god forbid
I'm looking at the cracked earth Aborigines
Made love with, because earth is god,
I'm watching and I'm not looking for anything
anymore

WHY I BECAME AN ACTIVIST

Judy Hogan

In 1998, I had finally found a small home I could afford. I'd searched the whole Triangle area of North Carolina. I needed to be within twenty-five miles of Chapel Hill and Durham, where I had friends and work. I had discovered that a low-level nuclear dump had been planned for the Moncure area, but I decided to buy the house and land and work against it as my new neighbors had been doing for ten years. We stopped it, shortly after I moved in late 1998.

But there were other problems. A particle board plant was emitting more formaldehyde than any similar plant in the country. People were getting pneumonia, asthma; dogs let out at night came in with watering eyes. We fussed to our county commissioners (BoC) who summoned the state Department of Environment and Natural Resources (DENR). Their representative claimed they didn't want to hurt the company, and their vice president told me that formaldehyde dissipated in the air. Within three years, that plant was sold, and the new owners put in new machinery. People stopped getting sick.

Then we tried to stop the shipping of nuclear waste through Moncure. The train track goes by our post office, in the heart of our village. We spoke to our Chatham County Board of Commissioners. I had called our local fire department and asked what they would do if a train carrying nuclear waste wrecked in Moncure. They had no idea. So, the BoC voted to complain to the state attorneys general and did. Progress Energy, formerly CP&L, now Duke Energy, said they'd stop shipping the waste in two years. Did they? I've never been sure.

Then came county elections. The BoC was a key player when we fought pollution. I worked for our president, Mike Cross. He'd helped with the formaldehyde problem. He was elected in 2004. By 2010, I helped elect all five members of the BoC, who were standing firm to keep down polluting industries and keep out unexamined residential development. I was ready to take a break from so much activism.

I'm a writer, and I wanted more time for my books, where I was putting my experiences in these various fights for clean air, water, land, but, in 2012, here came the threat of fracking. I joined with activists in our neighboring Lee County, where a small amount of gas existed, and was not far from my home. I worked, too, with the Haw River Assembly to put up signs. I went door to door with petitions. In my mostly Black neighborhood, everybody signed. Finally, the fracking fight moved to the courtroom and slowed down.

I thought I could stop all this, but again, in 2014, a good friend called me to announce that sixty trucks a day would be bringing coal ash from the Wilmington and Charlotte areas past my home. Then Elaine Chiosso of the Haw River Assembly wanted my help to call a meeting. So, we began our long struggle to stop the dumping of coal ash in our Moncure community. Coal ash hasn't so far been declared hazardous by the EPA, but it does kill people slowly. We have lost four of our activists to cancer in recent years.

By April 2015, I had become the chair of our Chatham Citizens Against Coal Ash Dump (CCACAD). We hired a lawyer to challenge the permits, which were rushed through, and this time the BoC was prohibited by law from interfering. Duke Energy even made a deal with our BoC, to give them $19 million for taking 12 million tons of coal ash. Mike Cross, still on the BoC, led the commissioners to sign the deal, and three of the five did. When he came to our meeting to explain his reasoning, someone hissed, "Traitor," and I asked them to hold their comments until Mike spoke. When he finished, I said to him, "I don't trust you anymore, Mike." He has refused to look at me ever since.

They called our coal ash dump a "mine reclamation," but even the EPA said it was merely a landfill. We had gone to open hearings with information about how landfills always leak, how twelve kinds of bacteria eat the plastic liner that holds the coal ash in place. They claimed it would last five-hundred years, and buildings could be sited on top of it. Hardly. In court we lost in the Office of Administrative Hearings, then won in the Superior court. They were to stop digging new holes. But, the Appeals Court allowed Charah, the coal ash management company, a "stay," so they didn't have to obey the Superior Court and stop digging.

Finally, the Appeals Court sent us back to the Office of Administrative Hearings and the Superior Court, claiming both those judges did it wrong. As it turned out the OAH judge, Lassiter, ruled in our favor this time. Charah's appeal of that decision is delayed because of the pandemic.

Meantime, in the fall of 2018, we had two hurricanes passing over us, after days of rain. The coal ash "reclamation" was inundated with red mud. Drone photos showed coal ash outside the cells. We heard that Charah was going to stop dumping ash at seven million tons, but we don't know anything for sure. The permits are still challenged in court, but they still own the land in Chatham and Lee, and the permits are still good at the moment.

To add insult to injury, Duke Energy is building a STAR reprocessing plant nearby, which takes the carbon out of coal ash, making it suitable for cement. They will re-burn the coal ash in the five unlined ponds (5-1/2 million tons) which are, and have been, leaking into the Cape Fear River. These re-processing plants pollute the air every time they are turned on or off.

Moncure is sited where three rivers come together: The Haw and the Deep become the headwaters of the Cape Fear River, which flows to the North Carolina coast. These coal ash ponds next to the site of the old Cape Fear plant have been leaking for years into the rivers, polluting drinking water for about 500,000 people downstream. The intake for the Sanford Water Treatment plant is just below where the coal ash is leaking, and our southeastern Chatham's water comes from Sanford.

I'm still the chair of CCACAD and expect I will be as long as I can, but I've slowed down now at the age of eighty-three. Trains and trucks still go through our little community, and some coal ash dust is microscopic. You can't see it. But it can go straight to the brain. Some mornings I have wiped black specks off my truck's damp windows.

This community has been my home for over twenty years. I love these people, and I still believe we can stop it. It takes determination, work, and money. It takes love of each other to stand up to this kind of cruelty.

HOW BECOMING A GRANDMOTHER TURNED ME INTO AN ACTIVIST

Alexandra Grabbe

I looked down at Juliette, sleeping peacefully in my arms, and prayed she would not develop cancer or autism. I have always known about environmental contaminants, but now the consequences of pollution hit me full force. The 2006 birth of this precious baby, my first grandchild, changed my approach to the world. As the months passed, I realized her life would be a treacherous obstacle course with the avoidance of toxic chemicals as one of the biggest challenges. It was this state of affairs that turned me into an activist.

When I started a green bed & breakfast on Cape Cod in 2005, all my energy had gone into locating organic cotton sheets, non-toxic cleansers, and natural amenities. Juliette's existence pushed me onto another level of greenness, a plateau where I thought about the significance of these choices. Why are so many chemicals necessary for the manufacture of non-organic cotton–up to two-hundred, per plant, per season? Why would the United States government allow its citizens to use cleaning products that require a warning on the bottle to the effect that they may be dangerous to health? Why are parabens and synthetic fragrance added to most shampoos, lotions, and soaps? Why had it become necessary to search out organic food and vegetables in order to avoid pesticide residue? Slowly I began to question the status quo because the future of my grandchild was at stake.

My transformation did not occur overnight. I started paying closer attention to investigative reporting on PBS. Public television had already increased my awareness of body burden in 2003, after Bill Moyers expressed shock at the number of chemicals found in his own blood. I read articles on pollution and discovered DEET had been detected in municipal water in Chicago. I learned of the existence of endocrine disruptors, chemicals that disrupt the hormones in our bodies. Then I listened to Terry Gross on NPR's *Fresh Air*, interviewing Charles Duhigg, who recommended the use of a filter for tap water. I had tuned in after reading Duhigg's report in *The New York Times* about water contamination in the Midwest caused by the widely used herbicide Atrazine. A grandmother looks at the world through a different lens. What I saw was deplorable.

Juliette exchanged her diapers for frilly cotton dresses. As she became a little girl, I kept asking questions. How can farmers give cows artificial growth hormones, so people drink a toxic brew rather than the pure milk consumed by our ancestors? Why did the government allow thousands of toxic chemicals to enter the environment without regulation? How was no attention paid to the content of personal care products before they went on the market? How did flame-retardants (PBDEs) get into dust? How could perchlorate, a jet fuel additive, show up in breast milk? Was there no thought to the lives of firefighters who use fire-fighting foam containing PFAS? How was it possible to permit the application of bisphenol A (BPA) to sales receipts, not to mention baby bottles and the lining of canned goods? Why had no one linked the phenomenal increase in cancer to the toxic chemicals that are now pervasive in our environment?

"Just one thing of which you must beware: don't drink the water and don't breathe the air," sang Tom Lehrer on his album *That Was the Year That Was*, recorded in 1967. No longer could this song about the effects of pollution be laughed off. While I was raising my own children, Love Canal happened. The Cuyahoga River in Cleveland caught fire. Erin Brockovich brought down a California power company that was polluting a city's water supply. The fact that industry was willing to disregard pollution proved corporate greed trumped good sense. The God of Money reigned, even on Capitol Hill where decisions are supposed to be made with the welfare of We the People in mind.

When the Environmental Working Group tested the umbilical cord blood of ten women in 2009, researchers found 300 chemicals, including BPA, perchlorate, and PFDEs. I found this outrageous.

According to the Environmental Health Trust, the incidence of cancer has increased 48% from 1950 to 1990. Today one in eight women will develop breast cancer during her lifetime. One in fifty-nine American children will show symptoms of autism, according to the CDC.

Here on Cape Cod, the utility company sprays five toxic chemicals, including glyphosate, under our power lines. Federal law does not mandate the use of chemicals. It only requires the removal of new vegetation. In the past, the utility company relied on mowing.

For ten years, a group of concerned citizens tried to stop the madness. We suggested goats, but the utility clung to its original plan. Cape Cod has very sandy soil. The herbicides filter down into our sole source aquifer. Traces end up in private wells and drinking water. So far, we have not won this battle. Although glyphosate has been declared a carcinogen by the state of California, in Massachusetts people can still spray herbicides whenever they want.

In 2008, the EPA released a list of 104 "priority drinking water contaminants for regulatory consideration," chosen "based on their potential to pose health risks through drinking water exposure." By the time President Obama signed the Frank R. Lautenberg Chemical Safety for the 21st Century Act, which updated the Toxic Substances Control Act, the chemical industry had weighed in. The bill Congress passed was a watered-down version of the one Senator Lautenberg had imagined prior to his untimely death.

Juliette is now thirteen. I have three other grandchildren. I have not succeeded in stopping the pollution of the Cape Cod sole source aquifer and, with the current EPA, laws for toxic chemicals have become even more lax. Still, I speak out. I buy organic. I warn strangers about toxins in water. I give my bed-and-breakfast guests a copy of Dr. Theo Colborn's *Our Stolen Future*.

The fact remains: chemicals are polluting the environment and endangering health. The welfare of future generations is at stake. It's time to put two and two together. Toxic chemicals + food + water = people with disease. For Juliette's sake, I protest. You may not be a grandmother yet, but I invite you to join me. Get outraged.

MAKING A DIFFERENCE BY IMPLEMENTING IMPORTANT PUBLIC PROJECTS

Leslie Penelope Recht

For as long as I can remember, I have been interested in politics. I have lived my entire life in the city of Chicago, so that defined the boundaries of local politics for me.

My mom was a good government crusader, and when I was young, that meant that she was fighting against the Daley machine. Her anger was focused on political corruption. She was angry at precinct captains who promised services for votes, using new garbage cans or reductions in property taxes, and she wanted to work to end the easy corruption that pervaded politics in Chicago. I watched and learned as my mom became more active and vocal, bringing me along as she worked on campaigns and supported candidates who she hoped could change the system.

My dad was a statistician working for the National Safety Council. His motivations included a passion to make a difference in public policy, for instance providing the data to Congress to support the 55 mph interstate highway speed limit. My dad worked with many at the state and local levels, through a not-for-profit that was strong because it was supported by both governmental and business partners.

In college, I had a chance to refine my thinking away from my parents, and my thinking evolved so that my opinions no longer matched their opinions on many particular issues. However, I found my most enjoyable classes and activities related to political science, urban studies, and public policy. That is still true today. I believe that is due in large part to my parents' influence and examples, but also my own strong need to be of service and to support what is fair and equitable.

I was not sure what I wanted to do after college, so I took a year off to work and to explore possibilities. I was interested in administrative law and got a clerk's job at a state agency under Governor Richard B. Ogilvie, who was bringing extraordinary reforms to state government. I had friends and a spouse who served in Ogilvie's administration and had a front row seat to see how politics and government administration interrelated, including the good, the corrupt, and the sloppy.

Cleaning up the mess from past administrations was exhilarating. Watching new public policy initiatives, like the first environmental department, before the federal EPA, showed me what could be done. This only confirmed my career interest to become an attorney concentrating on public policy issues. I enjoyed reading, writing and arguing, so despite the strong bias against admitting women to law school in the early 1970s, I persevered and was admitted with 11 other women and I graduated with high honors from law school, Chicago-Kent College of Law at the Illinois Institute of Technology.

During law school, I had the opportunity to clerk for an inspirational judge in the Circuit Court and clerked in the appeals division of the legal department of the City of Chicago, participating in fascinating cases on the new Illinois constitution and many issues of public importance. I took public policy classes in law school on environmental law, a new area then, and product liability. I was intent on making a difference and got a job with Peoples Energy that involved administrative law, litigation and public policy in the energy field at the state and local levels.

I found that practicing law could be all-consuming. I continued practicing as an energy attorney with private firms, but I had very little time for personal activities during the early years of my practice. However, after five years, I began to engage in volunteer work.

Volunteering for committee and officer positions at various bar associations was enjoyable, but it was an extension of my practice. I was a frustrated urban planner, so I sought positions where I could learn about what was being planned in Chicago and weigh in through good government groups. I participated through Friends of Downtown Chicago in reviewing proposed real estate and public developments. My interest in parks grew, so I represented Friends of Downtown in a consortium of groups that worked on a range of public policy issues and commented as a group on proposals to governmental agencies. This consortium included Friends of the Parks and the Metropolitan Planning Council, among others. I saw that joint, concerted action was an effective way to make some incremental changes, but I also saw the limitations of those groups. They had no authority to make decisions — they were only advisory and were primarily strong through their ability to provide technical analysis and to muster public opinion.

I started to act on my own, founding the Grant Park Advisory Council in the mid-1990s. At that time, Grant Park was scarred by large outdoor parking lots along the Illinois Central railroad tracks between Monroe and Randolph, and the Park District was floating ideas about decking over the railroad tracks and expanding the park. It was exciting to become involved in these planning efforts, to have a voice at the table and to watch as famous urban planners like Larry Halprin were called in to facilitate the planning process for all stakeholders. Lake Shore Drive was moved from east to west of the Field Museum of Natural History to create what is now the Museum Campus.

These efforts often resulted in drama. I supported closing Meigs Field, the small lakefront airport, for environmental, noise and safety reasons, and cheered when that was done. The Grant Park Advisory Council was a raucous place that included some very self-interested members who had figured out ways to make money on the side from the Park. As my law practice became busier and I was traveling a lot, it became more difficult to stay active in my volunteer roles. There is a life span to many of these volunteer groups, and it was reasonable for me to step back from my advocacy in Grant Park.

I did find time to stay active in my neighborhood on the Near West Side, serving on the advisory council for my local park and working with neighborhood associations on planning issues related to development, parking, and zoning. It was always important to work with my alderman and these associations because so many issues impacted me, my neighborhood, and my welfare and safety.

After practicing law for almost thirty-five years, I retired from my law practice to work for eight years for a progressive Chicago alderman, Bob Fioretti. I was a volunteer who worked 20-30 hours each week, concentrating primarily on schools, parks and Chicago Housing Authority issues. We had a ward with 80,000 people on the Near South Lakefront, then going west on both sides of the Eisenhower Expressway. We had forty Chicago public schools in our ward, twenty-three parks when we started, adding or expanding five parks the first four years and five more parks the second four years.

The ward had a lot of commercial and manufacturing areas being converted to residential development in the South and West Loop, so we were building necessary neighborhood infrastructure, including many new parks. Several of these parks had new dog-friendly areas and one included an indoor children's play area. We used Tax Increment Financing (TIF) to fund major improvements to parks and to build or renovate magnet schools, which included a priority for students who were living within the area around the schools for the first time. I took the public policy lead in the processes that we used for coordinating with City, Park District, CPS and other agencies as we held neighborhood forums and received input on all of these efforts.

We named two parks for women, Mary Bartelme, named for an amazing trailblazing judge, and Bertha Honore Palmer, who was President of the Board of Lady Managers of the 1893 World's Columbian Exposition in Chicago and donated an extensive collection of important impressionist art to the Art Institute of Chicago.

Very few parks in Chicago are named for women, and this effort to recognize and acknowledge women was very important to me. I was also able to finish the creation and installation of a major permanent exhibit of photos of famous Chicago women at Chicago Women's Park and Gardens, along with a booklet of bios of 64 famous Chicago women. This was a culmination of the intention of naming a park for famous Chicago women, to see that they are celebrated and their accomplishments are remembered.

These experiences showed me the power of working within the system with aldermen who believed in the proper use of TIFs and the use of community engagement. The effectiveness of this work was based on the aldermanic authority to approve projects and the use of governmental funds. This work took patience, a lot of time and creativity, and a team approach engaging governmental officials and members of the community.

I also helped to establish or re-establish park advisory councils, supported local school councils and with my alderman fought against school closings that were extremely difficult for our residents. We established joint task forces between representatives of the Chicago Police Department, Chicago Public Schools and the Chicago Transit Authority and several wards to work on school violence.

I was lucky to be able to work with aldermen who shared my values in so many public policy areas. What I found was that it is much more effective to work for government at a time when we were able to make changes that improved the lives of our residents so significantly. Without the TIFs and the other funding we had available, we would not have been able to improve those communities so significantly.

I ended my city service after eight years and took a break from politics and volunteer work. For me, it was important to regroup and to reassess my priorities and time commitments.

Some friends convinced me to return to public service by asking me to help them investigate the situation at the Grant Park Advisory Council in 2016. After much discussion and lobbying, our efforts resulted in a report by the Chicago Park District Inspector General about the council and its leadership. Based on this report, the park district reorganized the Grant Park Advisory Council. In 2019, I was elected President of the Grant Park Advisory Council, more than 20 years after I established the Council. We have officers who are leading neighborhood organizations around Grant Park. We have established open committees and are working with the park district and aldermen in the area to improve Grant Park in its roles as both a neighborhood and a regional park.

It feels as though I have come full circle in my work with Chicago parks. I have done other volunteer work in retirement, so I know that this is what feeds and stimulates me. I have received awards and accolades for my efforts, but that feels like the icing, not the cake. For me, the reward is seeing good things happen that are better for my efforts and leadership. My passions to make a difference, to make changes in our environment, to recognize excellence and to work cooperatively, have led me into many adventures and learning opportunities.

My path has not been easy. Today, it seems much more difficult to accomplish important projects. However, even in today's environment, I see ways to continue making progress.

NOT ALL GUNS BLAZING

Gerard Sarnat

Instead of *kvelling**
l'il victories: $144
class action's long
sought settlement

or $20.06 excess
medicine co-pay
a mail-order Rx
fought hard, lost

I oughta spend
our remaining
hours loving, connecting,
protecting our earth.

*Yiddish for expressing pride.

EDUCATIONAL JUSTICE

DAY ONE

Jacqueline Ruegg

Three a.m., sobbing on the bathroom floor.
Months of fear and hope come to a head
with terrifying news. Shattered heart,
broken trust. That niggling voice, unable
to be silenced, turned out to be correct.

Pre-selected outfit for today, pink
and floral, no longer appropriate.
Replaced, instead, with black cardigan
and navy shirt.

Room full of adults
streaming silent tears,
looking for answers we
may never have. Together
in sorrow but filled with
despair. This is no time for
stoicism we cannot
muster.

How do we face the 300 humans
about to come through the doors
filled with loss and betrayal? How
do we make them safe when we,
too, are lost?

We must find the strength, both together and
alone. We are safety and home. We share their
grief, they will see and know, we are human
and heartbroken, too, but we need to be
consistent, constant, comfort.

We believed in the others.
Hoped we mattered enough.
Only to have the idea of equality
yanked out from under us.
We cannot fail them, too, no
matter our pain.

We must use it to show them:
Here, we are safe.
Here, we are equal.
Here, we matter.

Here, we take our collective
terror and passion and pain
and keep on fighting.

LETTER TO C & T

Linda L. Elman

March 11, 2015

Dear Granddaughters,

Please allow me to share a little history with you.

Forty years ago today, Grandma was fired from her teaching job at Munster High School. The administration called me out of class and had me report to the principal's office. I was in a state of panic, thinking that Grandpa might have had an accident in the mill, or that your dad had been hurt at school. Instead, the superintendent told me that he would not be renewing my contract for the following school year. He had a pink slip in hand.

I asked why, but he replied that he was not prepared to give me an answer at that time. For the next two years, six months, and one day, we searched for those answers. (Auntie Iris was fired, too, as a "smokescreen" for the real reason.) Although we were highly regarded teachers with excellent evaluations, the administration claimed to need teachers licensed to teach at least two languages. We were only certified in one language—Spanish. The fact that our classes were full of students did not seem to matter.

The state of Indiana had passed legislation (PL 217) requiring school boards to negotiate salary and benefits with teachers; other working conditions were to be formally discussed with teacher representatives. I was the duly appointed chairperson of Munster's official discussion team. Over time it became apparent that the only reason the superintendent attended our meetings was to comply with the law. We found out that he never carried our concerns to the school board. Once, in a professional meeting with my team, the superintendent looked at me and said, "You remind me a lot of my wife. Bitch. Bitch. Bitch."

One issue in particular was a priority for the teachers. We asked for one paid day at the start of school to get ready for our students. Typically, the first day back was filled with keynote speeches, principals' meetings, and a luncheon. There was no time to run off materials, unpack books, decorate classrooms, or hold department meetings. We needed this extra day. I wrote a letter to the school board members and delivered it directly to their homes, because our official channel to the board, our superintendent, was not communicating our request. When there was no response, I wrote an open letter to the community that appeared on March 8th in the local paper. On March 11th, we received notices stating that our contracts were not renewed. Effectively, with those contracts, we would have been given tenure in the school system.

With the help of our state and national associations (unions), Iris and I fought for our jobs. The administration claimed that there was no connection between March 8th (the letter) and March 11th (the dismissal). At each hearing, the decision was made in our favor and against the school administration. Ugly things came out at our hearings. For example, our superintendent told our high school principal, "Elman is like cancer of the leg and needs to be cut off before she infects the entire system." Our principal, who testified under oath to this comment in September, was summarily fired from his job the next spring. The battle dragged through the judicial system, ending in Circuit Court in Jasper County on July 7, 1977. Again, we won the case, but the school board voted to appeal the decision.

Finally, with pressure on the board from the community and teachers, we were able to come to a settlement. We were reinstated to our positions in October of 1977, with two years lost experience restored to our record and most of our back salary repaid. The two administrators charged with illegal activities under the law were ordered to "cease and desist" from unfair labor practices. The judge ordered that the legal decree be posted in all the Munster schools. Our case can be found in the Indiana statutes.

I was very proud to stand at the door to my classroom again, and I continued to teach at Munster High School until I retired in 1998. I fought for my rights under the law and for what I knew to be fair and just for teachers. It was never easy to maintain the fight, but in the end, justice prevailed for me, for Iris, for the Munster teachers, and for all Indiana teachers, because the PL217 had been tested and defended successfully.

If you are ever faced with unjust treatment, I hope you will find the inner courage to stand up for your convictions.

Love,
Grandma

WHY DOES IT HURT SO MUCH?

Deirdre L. Clawson

I have never cried at school before; I'm a big girl. Mother told me to keep my chin up and push forward. But today is different. I am standing in the restroom by the school's main office. I am cramped between a sink and two stalls attempting to hold back my tears, but I can't. A boy said something mean, very mean to me. I have never cried at school before. But this time is different.

This time it happened in my room, the room with my name on the door—my classroom—my space. It went like this, minutes after viewing a 23-minute film introducing the life of Frederick Douglass, an American hero, a student announces very loudly amidst the end-of-day chair stacking and student chatter, "As far as I'm concerned, slavery should have never been abolished; only about 5-percent of them ever do anything with their lives anyway." I sat in my chair stunned signaling the student who stood above me to stop talking while I listened. There was more, but I could not hear it.

This is the turning point for me. He has violated me in my space. I call him over and angrily give him my family history and explain that his insult was beyond belief and would never be tolerated— and he needed to report to the office. What made this sixteen-year-old boy so comfortable that he felt free to make these particular inaccurate racist remarks in my presence, and why did it hurt so much?

Upon reflection, I realize that this experience is just one painful example of a shift in the American narrative on racial equality, the racial divide, and the anger evoked by those who hate to see any group—other than their own—attempt to fully realize their American Dream. This shift is further demonstrated when teenagers can so blatantly declare that: the Holocaust did not happen, that slavery isn't worth learning about because they did not do it, affirmative action means that when a minority applies for a job along with a non-minority that the minority always gets the job. In their fantasy fiction journals, they want to return to slavery and control African Americans as it was "meant to be." From the mouths of babes, I have learned why it is so easy for Trump to ignite the masses and why it was so easy for Zimmerman to "stand his ground," and Paula Dean to have no remorse for her racist remarks because she "is what she is." I can go and say that I am not surprised to see law officers empowered to shoot and kill young black men in Chicago, Baltimore, Cleveland, New York, Dayton, Ferguson, and Dallas—just to name the most memorable acts of barbarity. Then the quintessential demonstration and most savage act of racism: the shooting of worshipers at the Emanuel African Methodist Episcopal Church in Charleston, an act which still leaves our nation confused and deeply wounded.

Further, instead of supporting and celebrating the country's first African American president as proof that the Constitution and affirmative action work, many resented Barack Obama's power. I suggest that the current attack on young Black men is and will always be a violent backlash to people of color who dared step foot in "their" White House. Just as my students' resentment to my authority in the classroom and reading literature about other cultures and races result in malicious remarks on social media. Instead of accepting that I celebrate the accomplishments of my culture, they label me a racist, and continue, to this day, on social media, to circulate racist remarks about me and call me a nigger, but why does it hurt so much?

I was even more shocked to discover that the discourse of ignorance and prejudice snakes throughout the classrooms and into the teachers' lounge. During a discussion about how the rising cost of college makes it difficult for many of our students to attend four-year institutions, a colleague and friend remarks: "Well Deirdre, didn't you get your college paid for through affirmative action?"

Days and days later when the shock subsides, I explain that being a Black college student back in the 1970s did not automatically qualify one for free tuition. I tell her that both my parents had jobs; my dad worked at GE for decades. Government money then and now goes to those who are in need, and my family was never in need. Like everyone else at that time, I got low-interest loans and I worked a college work-study job for four years. She stood, as the daughter of an injured veteran and the recipient of a fully financed college education, still perplexed; I stood again wondering, why did it hurt so much?

Another day, during our 25-minute lunch break, when I cannot identify a young rapper, a twenty something co-worker responds with, "Deirdre, I even know who he is and I'm white."

So, I say to myself, I am supposed to know the name of every rapper because I'm Black? What I do know is my culture and history, and that to this day, I can recite some of Gil Scott Heron's "H2O Gate Blues" and much of Grand Master Flash's protest rhyme exemplifying the cyclical plight of urban poverty — would that be environmental determinism? What I do know is that rap is music and hip-hop a cultural movement and that Langston Hughes's Bebop poetry was the precursor to hip-hop and therefore Hughes can be considered the first hip-hop artist. But, what I do not know is, why did it hurt so much?

In this new 21st century, post-affirmative action form of racism, students are empowered by divisive media that hurls misinformation using hostile rhetoric and a president who spews hate. They are stifled by lack of sensitivity, lack of connectivity to the real world, lack of contact with others outside their segregated neighborhoods. So, they label me, their only African American teacher, and my passionate messages of pride and diversity as exemplified through literature I teach — a "racist." They strike out by starting a Facebook page titled "Clawson's Racist" with a goal to "get me out." The ultimate show of this newly empowered racism was maximized when a triad of students left to their own devices in a classroom, made a full-fledged mural depicting the KKK, nooses, a tombstone with the name of our nation's first Black leader, RIP (Rest In Peace) nigger then posted it proudly on Twitter. It becomes very clear.

I had never planned on being a teacher when I was younger. When I went through the undergraduate program at Spelman College in the mid-1970s, students encouraged to join the ranks of Corporate America had finally left the door ajar for a few of us. After spending a lackluster decade and a half as an account representative for a few major corporations, I decided to respond to President Clinton's call for teachers. People who wanted to make a difference in the country — it was and still is a fit. I certainly never expected to experience either the overt racism of ignorant children or the micro-aggressions of educated adults. This is why it hurts so much — my vision of a "mo' better America" has turned to salt as she ungraciously turns to look and laugh at the down and out, persecute the unfamiliar, and curse the changing American demographics. Will the universe provide justice and open the sea to swallow those who are hell-bent on denying the pursuit of happiness to all Americans?

To these pressing questions, perhaps the answer is clear. That's why, in fact, it did and does hurt so much. Perhaps this confusion and fear is best described as a premonition or best compared to how one feels when an accident is eminent — the terror after the skid — the loss of control as the car begins spinning into its second 360-degree circle moments before a crash that could in fact leave some dead. Fear.

I fear that if America does not soon fix this problem, she will surely fail. She is a country of immigrants in the midst of global expansion; she cannot afford to encourage her citizens to hate one another. This division and hatred will eventually result in the decline of the greatest nation ever established, destroying our position as the world's leader in the fight for democracy.

Nonviolently, Martin Luther King insisted that America make good on the tenets of our great Constitution, that "all men are created equal . . . and have the right to life, liberty, and the pursuit of happiness." It is my responsibility; it is your responsibility to make every American scream, "Justice and liberty for all!" It is time to scream about the 1-percent at the top who control this nation, just as the lords controlled Europe when the original immigrants decided to flee. We must begin to diagnose racism's severe impact on individuals, families, communities. Perhaps then the nation, and finally the world will design, write, and implement the prescription to cure this modern, blatant strain of America's most painful plague — racism — fueled by violently charged, divisive rhetoric.

NOTE: When I began teaching at a former vocational-technical high school located in a modest blue-collar neighborhood, the demographics and attitudes were quite different from what they are today. Those were days before the arrival of the determined, gritty immigrant population, before Obama was elected president, and well before hatefulness became a national pastime. The school was 75% white; I was the only teacher of color. The climate of the school community, both teachers and students, was majority-focused, minority insensitive. Both groups enjoyed their white privilege without ever admitting or understanding its existence. Needless to say, those first years were a challenge. I wrote the essay, "Why does It Hurt So Much?" in response to a painful encounter: one that "broke my back," so to speak. Later, on the same day of this incident, I was commended for my work in promoting diversity in the classroom by the Muslim Community Support Services.

Fast forward to 2017 when a group of three-hundred angry students staged a silent sit-in in response to a racial slur etched on the baseball field. I thought that it was time to share my story. But, more importantly, I needed to calm, guide, and model how to react to hatred in a respectful, non-violent manner. I shared my pain and my still open wounds. What came next was a day-long testimonial with literally hundreds of students sharing their stories. From this day, a "Stay Woke" group was formed. I continue to help them find their voices.

THEY DON'T SEE US

Sharron Goodman-Hill

As a second-year graduate student, I was privileged to view a documentary titled *Wanda Jacobs: Making History and Headlines*. This documentary highlighted the career of an African American woman who became first Black and female publisher of *The Sun Press* in Pascagoula, Mississippi. In this video Wanda Jacobs pointed out that the photographers and editors at that time often used pictures of whites when they could have just as easily used pictures of Blacks. One day there were pictures of white children playing in a park included in the newspaper. The pictures were not associated with any story. These were just pictures that the editor decided to use to fill a particular page. Jacobs asked her mostly white staff if there were any Black children at the park. According to Jacobs, this question stunned her staff. They could not answer her because they honestly did not have an answer that would justify their reason for not automatically including African Americans in their random photos. Jacobs stated that the photographers and editors did not include Blacks because, "They don't see us..."

This historical video, produced by Ralph Braseth, was so impactful on my life, particularly this portion. They don't see us. They don't see us. They don't see us. They simply don't see us. So, after viewing this video, I periodically went on a personal crusade for journalistic representation justice.

Shortly after viewing the documentary, a publisher from Pontotoc, Mississippi, came to visit a class I was enrolled in at the University of Mississippi. He gave a brief presentation and brought myriad newspapers that he proudly displayed.

There were old bound copies of his paper that dated back centuries up to recent newspapers. As I browsed all of the newspapers, I noticed the complete absence of Black people in this broad array of newspapers. I thought that perhaps no Blacks were in the archival papers because, let's face it, they didn't see us. We were never intended to be citizens of this great country. Why would they see us? I continued my perusal of what seemed to be our guest's pride and joy. The search was to no avail. There were simply no Blacks in these newspapers. I had put it off for as long as I could. I had to ask. I knew it would make our guest, who had gotten up extremely early to make the early trek on a hot summer morning, uncomfortable, but I knew I had to ask. "Do African Americans not make the news in Pontotoc?" There! I asked the one million dollar question. I asked the question....the unavoidable question that I had to ask, especially in light of the fact that I had been recently enlightened after viewing the Jacobs documentary. I was the only African American in that class. If I did not say anything, no one else would.

Although it was only a few seconds, it seemed like an eternity as my classmates and I waited for the guest publisher to respond to the question regarding Black representation in the Pontotoc newspaper. Through a red face and several incomplete sentences and incoherent words, the publisher retorted, "I guess not...maybe in the sports section." He was digging himself deeper in a hole. In those few words, he confirmed what publisher Wanda Jacobs said... they don't see us. His response explained why Black communities have had to create their own newspapers because if not, people of color would not have been placed in mainstream media for anything of positive substance. He had no idea how offensive and stereotypical his blunt answer had been.

My hope is that no matter where the students in the classroom that day ended up, my question helped them become aware that diversity and inclusion are important in every capacity. I further hope that the guest publisher went back to Pontotoc knowing and believing that people of color deserve positive, prominent media influence in his hometown. I also hope that my professor, who co-produced the Jacobs documentary that inspired me to ask that tough question in 1995, became more conscious. I hope it motivated him to make sure people from all walks of life would be included in whatever media he engages in producing.

This was the beginning of my role as a foot soldier for journalism justice in my own small way. I want people to see us... not just for crime or even sports, but for the contributions that African Americans make daily which impact the greater good in our society. There have been several times over the years when I made small footprints for journalistic justice. For the purposes of space, I am highlighting a few.

After graduating from the University of Mississippi, I matriculated at the University of Memphis and as a class requirement, I authored a paper titled, "A Picture is Worth a Thousand Words." This research was inspired from the Pontotoc, Mississippi newspaper publisher visit. At that time, Holly Springs, Mississippi was blessed with two newspapers; *The South Reporter*, which began in 1865, and *The Marshall Chronicle*, a newspaper geared toward the African American audience that began in the early 2000s and only lasted a few years. I hypothesized that African Americans would not be featured on the front page of the town's mainstream, long-time established newspaper unless it was a story about sports, politics, or crime. And, if they were on the front page, the pictures would be below the fold.

Four weeks of each newspaper were used for this research. While my hypotheses were disproved for this brief study, they still drew attention to the fact that Black people are often featured negatively, especially in small-town newspapers. It garnered attention in class, a chance to apply to present the research at a conference for Southern journalists and on campus at University of Memphis. It was definitely a pebble thrown into a pond that caused a few ripples and ruffled a few feathers.

The absence of African Americans in pictures is not just limited to newspapers, broadcast media, etc. That absence can be seen on college campuses in subtle ways even though integration may have taken place many years ago. Let's take East Central Community College in my hometown of Decatur, Mississippi. Decatur is also the hometown of civil rights icons, the late State NAACP Field Secretary Medgar Evers, and his elder brother, Charles Evers. The elder Evers went on to become the first African American mayor of Fayette, Mississippi and many other great accomplishments in his life span. They both graduated from Alcorn State University. Now why did the Evers Brothers not attend ECCC, then known as East Central Junior College? It was probably because Blacks did not enter those doors as students at that time. Integration for Black students at ECCC did not take place until 1970 with Glenda Nichols, Patricia Reese and a few other brave souls. As southern African American preachers often say in their sermons, "Stick with me. I'm going somewhere with this!"

I accompanied my oldest daughter, Victoria, to college orientation in summer 2004 to prepare for her intended matriculation at ECCC in that upcoming fall semester. I believe my daughter selected this school for sentimental reasons; one being that my father passed away a few months earlier that same year. Whatever the reason, we were there to begin her college career. As I sat with my daughter, I began to get a sinking feeling in my gut. Not one Black person got up to present anything. My daughter had grown up watching people who look similar to her in leading roles on a college campus. She basically had grown up on an HBCU campus. Her middle and high schools were predominately black. The towns where her formative years were spent were also highly populated by African Americans. To go from what she considered the norm to not seeing any Blacks in leadership that morning at ECCC was disturbing for me as well as for my daughter. To add insult to injury, I began to look around this massive auditorium and noticed pictures hanging beautifully, but there were no African Americans on these pictures.

As we recessed to head to another session and as fate would have it, the president of the college himself passed by. We spoke and I engaged him in conversation. I commented on how nice the photographs were. We were then in the college's cafeteria area where even larger, spectacularly clear and colorful photos of college scenes were displayed and not one Black person on any of them! The college president began to boast about the college's Public Relations Department and the work of his capable PR staff. I interjected, "I don't see any African Americans on these pictures."

He looked around the room at these award-worthy photographs and he could not point to one of the many African Americans who attended this thriving institution of education on those prominently displayed pictures.

Decades had passed since the first Blacks integrated this school; thirty-four years to be exact and they still did not see us. I happened to be one of those students having matriculated at ECJC in 1978 and graduated in 1980. I returned in 1985 while pregnant with Victoria in the summer and fall terms of 1985. This time around I founded the ECCC Gospel Choir, finally made the President's List, and participated in many other extracurricular activities, but yet they did not see me…they didn't see us.

Former US First Lady Michelle Obama bravely stated while on the campaign trail with her husband in 2008, "For the first time in my adult life, I am really proud of my country because it feels like hope is finally making a comeback." For months on end, Mrs. Obama was raked over the coals by mainstream media about her statement. My thought on this dynamic was and still is not only do they not see us, but they do not understand us when we speak our truths and realities... when we voice our concerns about what it is like to be overlooked, to be excluded... what it is like to be Black in America.

Soledad O'Brien did an incredible job with the CNN docu-series *Black in America*. I had such high hopes and anticipation for this show. However, after viewing it I felt deflated and defeated and I was left with my thought, "They still do not know what it's like to be Black in America. THEY STILL DON'T SEE US!

Thank God for Samuel Cornish and John Brown Russwurm who are credited for creating the first African American newspaper *Freedom's Journal*. Thank God for Frederick Douglass's *The North Star* and for Ida B. Wells becoming part-owner of the Memphis *Free Speech* in 1892. These newspapers and several others gave a platform for Black people to see themselves on the high society pages. They gave way to Black Americans having the right to bring attention to injustices that mainstream media overlooked. After all, they (mainstream media) did not and still do not see us!

PUNCHING BAG

Chad W. Lutz

swing low America
punch whatever ails
squarely in the gut

twist the fist
make the belly bleed

internal yearning
might make
things better

but
sods in office
will always be

that's why we must
stick our heads out
our windows &
clamor for
the changing of times

strike up a racket
textbooks years
from now can only document

& never know the full
truth of sound

THE BODY OF THE ESSAY

CMarie Fuhrman

I woke up this morning preparing an apology. I am in my final year of an MFA. I have missed my writing workshop three times in a row. Haven't had the opportunity to talk in person to my classmates about their work, even though I have gotten to read and comment on it. Now my own essay is a week late. And that essay, though nineteen pages, is rife with typographical errors. Has a repeated paragraph. I only had the chance to make one revision. I was feeling as if somehow I had let them down.

The first thing I had not expected to happen during my MFA career was to still be taking classes. I had front-loaded heavily so that I would not have to make the commute in the last year of the program and fulfill my thesis credits from home. Write with my dogs beside me. A fire in the stove. Caleb across from me at dinner every night, within arm's reach in bed.

The second was to have a job I love and feel is important: my work for Native students in education goes far beyond me, into the third and fourth generations of students that my students will teach. Every day that I sit down to do that work, I am changing the world, in my small way, for Indian kids. This job has changed me, changed my life.

Last week, I traveled to Santa Fe. On Thursday morning, I was invited to Nambe Pueblo to the Feast of St Francis de Assisi. There would be dances there in the plaza. At noon a huge feast in every home. I arrived in time to hear the drums and watch dust rise from moccasined and tennis-shoed feet. Men in ribbon shirts dazzled in the sun. Women danced wearing the colors of the desert in bloom. Afterward, I was invited to lunch in the house of Picuris and Nambe family. I was seated across from Kelly, a Picuris elder. He was toothless. Ninety-three. A Vietnam vet. His laughter was the morning.

After telling me a story about a man who goes up a ladder and keeps falling back down, he asks me what I do. I tell him. I work in Native education. I work for higher education. That I am here in New Mexico to finish an anthology of Native poetry, craft, and ancestor texts. That in the morning I will go to Santa Fe Indian School and tell them that we will take their high school graduates, educate them with Indigenous pedagogies. I will invite some of their teachers to visit us. To share with our students. Then, as often happens in the aura of a witnessing presence, I begin to unload everything. I tell him that I am a writer. That I am an activist with my poetry. I write about Native women. Our bodies. I tell him about my students. I tell him about our program, that it brings this, I gestured to the plaza and to the table and people, culture, into the education of educators. It keeps culture in education. Native ways of knowing. And I tell him about the week before when I was in Montana with an audience of well-meaning white folk, and me, the organizer of a panel about Decolonizing Mythologies of the West. The often incorrect way that Native people are represented in literature. How it has to stop.

Has to stop.

I tell him that I got up to speak and that my grandmother was in my throat. Her grandmother. All my dead sisters. My aunties. They all wanted to talk to these white Montanans. So many voices that for a minute I could not speak.

I had to wait.

I had to ask my relatives for permission. When finally I spoke there was the end of winter in my voice.

I told him that I joined committees on my campus to change what happens for Native writers, for Native students that will come behind me, and then I told him of trees, of a lake in the Wilderness, of my dogs and my partner and that I was tired and sometimes I felt like I wanted to just toss it all in for something manageable. Easy. I told him that before I decided to go back to school I worked for a pizza place in the town I lived in. In McCall.

He sat silent for a moment. Nodding. He looked at me with eyes like shiny stones in a warm pool. He looked at me the way we should look into our own eyes when we peer back at them in the water. In a mirror. That kindness.

He said then, "You know how I know you are Indian?" It's an old joke.

I smiled and shook my head.

He said, "It's not your turquoise. It is not your long braids. It is not your skin. Or even some ID you might carry." He paused then.

"I know you are Indian, because you fight for Indians."

That phrase touched me like a finger to an important passage in a book. I sat with it for a minute. I had never thought about what I was doing as fighting. Being Native has meant that everything I do has been a little harder. A little more political. More highly observed, keenly judged. Being a Native woman has doubled that.

Before we had begun speaking, I was eating frybread. The wind had been blowing through the pueblo in which we sat. There were no lights, only sun through the arched and open door. Around us chatter continued. But I sat, frybread cooling between the fingers of my right hand. My eyes could not leave his. He extended his hands to me, palms up. I lay my bread down. Wiped the opulent grease from my fingers then put them in his.

He said, "Repeat after me." And in a language that only my bones knew, he spoke.

I echoed.

He said it again. And then his wife, who had, until this point been silent, also said it. I repeated. Down the table the two words were spoken in that soft Indian way. Like tanned deer hide. Like the shaft of a porcupine quill, but the point was not forgotten. I repeated it several times.

"It will give you strength," Kelly said. My hands were still in his. His hands warm and gentle. "You say it whenever you need strength. We will all say it with you. We fight with you. My time as a soldier didn't end in Vietnam and yours has only begun. Keep fighting for us."

We talked then about language. We talked about trees and about frybread and enchiladas. We ate with our fingers and we laughed.

"Indians can have very hard discussions," Kelly said, "but we always end with laughter." Then he told me a joke about General Custer.

⌷⌷⌷

Back at the University several days later, I was asked to talk about Native women in higher education. It was a video interview. Our cameras the eyes that watched us. Another Native woman in her office on a campus on the East Coast and me in mine. We started simply, where are you from? What degrees do you have? What are you doing now? We talked about IKEEP, the program that I coordinate. We talked about some of the struggles of my students. Then she asked about all the extracurricular work that I do. Outside the office. I told her. I told her that lately I have felt that my writing has suffered. I told her many of the things that I told Kelly, and I longed for the comfort again of his hands, balled my fingers up instead, kept them in my lap.

She sat back in her seat. Short ponytail lay like a sleeping dark mare across her tattooed shoulder. She collapsed in toward her chest. The interviewer was gone for a moment. And we sat, two Native women looking at each other over thousands of miles.

She said, "Educate and defend." She was repeating what I had answered when she asked what my time in higher education was like."You have described in two words my whole life."

Stephanie has her PhD., conducting interviews for her research on Native women in academia. She hopes to make higher education a better place for Native scholars. Trying to make more space, trying to bring awareness for the struggles of Natives, particularly Native women in higher education. I reflected her posture. I was two days off the road and one and a half more until I traveled again. My body was a field plowed too many times. My body was a sheet left on the line during a windstorm. My body was a battlefield on which skirmishes never stopped. Boot prints bruised my chest.

"We have to fight harder," she said at last. "As women, as Native women. To make it better."

I nodded. We thanked each other deeply for the work that we do and the connection ended. The small screen that held her images disappeared into the black and before me instead was the internal report I was writing for the Office of Indian Education. The explanation of how we have spent the money granted us. I was telling the story of my students' success in the dominate language of the country. Money.

I became aware again of another person in my office—a new hire, Angela. A white woman with a degree in natural resources and a desire to do work that mattered. I rubbed my eyes wondering what she thought of the conversation that she overheard. I didn't ask. I put my glasses back on and started typing. Words like persisters. Words like annuity. Phrases such as 89% success rate. 100% financial support.

At night, in the room that friends have made for me three and a half hours from the room where sits my family, I begin to read the story that I have submitted to my workshop group. It is rife with mistakes. Punctuation errors, grammar errors. Words entirely misspelled. A repeated paragraph. I had written the story in the Spokane Airport waiting for a flight. An hour later, 10,000 feet, I opened the file labeled "Barren," then a new Word document, and immediately started the rewrite. Halfway through I peered out my window unto lights in the desert. Utah. Maybe Nevada. I thought about prayers and dreams. How we were cutting through them in the night. Pressed into my seat between the cool beige of the airplane's interior and the sprawl of a young, white man who kept sleeping his head unto my shoulder, I rewrote a story about menopause. About bringing my blood into the earth with that of the women who came before me. About shedding the lining of my uterus and about how now, at nearly 50, I no longer had a reproductive choice. I was changing, moving into a third chapter in life. My body no longer a vessel for reproduction, but for something new. In the end, I wrote about swimming in a lake free of fish and frogs—its granite bottom—water like looking into a sapphire. Opening my eyes to a world I knew, then new again.

Back in my room, I put the piece down on my borrowed desk, unbraided my hair, traded black pants for my blue nightgown. A sigh like the wind before sunset left me. I am embarrassed by my work. That this essay was turned into my peers was a mistake. I needed to go through it at least once more. I thought of all the ways that I would apologize when I saw them the next day. I thought of my major professor. The way that he can look both disappointed and approving at the same time. I thought I should just drop the class. I crawled into the sheets and tried to find comfort on a futon mattress that held me like a child holds a rock, or a feather. I opened the book beside my bed, read until my mind let go of my mistakes. Dreamed about babies.

◻◻◻

I come to my journal upon waking. It is my routine. Wake, coffee, write. The journal entries are often filled with regret, plans for the day, full details of remembered dreams. Poems. Beginnings.

The essay. How would I explain to my classmates that it was not out of disrespect that I had missed three classes in a row? And it was also not a lack of respect for them or the craft which caused the errors in my writing. I could tell them about the road time driving. The air time. The young white man and his gin-sleep head falling again and again against mine making it harder and harder to write. The world moving below me. A backpack full of brochures for the Santa Fe Indian School between my feet. The hope that more students would want to become teachers on my calendar for Friday morning and 419 pages of an anthology called "Native Voices" to be finished in the mountains of New Mexico, in a place called Truchas, which over and over people tell me means trout, and I think that is not possible in a land that has no water.

I want to talk about the hours in my office. That I sometimes have three students studying in that small space, a chihuahua puppy in my desk drawer. That there are tears. That they come to me with syllabi that they cannot find themselves on. That they are writing about their life and their instructor gives them a poor grade because, the teacher will write, "I don't understand what you are trying to say." Do I have to say this to my classmates?

I woke up this morning after dreaming about babies, and I woke up not wanting to make an apology. I woke up thinking that I only had six hours of sleep, but that it did not matter. I felt Kelly's hands even as they were so far away: the warmth of that invisible rope that bound us. I repeated the words we said a week ago in the pueblo. I want to say to those who read the first draft of my essay that *this* is what it looks like to be a Native woman. But I stopped myself. And then I saw those mistakes as something other than errors. I saw them as proof of the work. Autobiographical artifacts. They were the laughter at the end of the difficult story.

We educate and we defend, I thought again as I closed my journal and made my way toward campus, toward my waiting classmates.

REPRESENTATION IN PUBLICATION

Leah Olajide

"Would you do this if you didn't make any money from it?" Keith asked.

"Yes," I answered sincerely and without hesitation.

My decision to move forward with *ColorBlind Magazine* was solidified.

That conversation happened in late 2011/early 2012 while talking to my cousin Keith. I love my cousin. We are both left-handed, Creatives, and Summer Babies although 10 years apart in age. I knew I couldn't share my plans for *ColorBlind Magazine* with just anyone, but I knew my idea for my publication was safe with him.

I wanted *ColorBlind Magazine* to be a publication that shared the struggles and celebrated the success of historical and contemporary women of color. Since its online debut in October 2012, *ColorBlind* has provided me with a unique platform that has expanded to include women of all races and backgrounds, but still keeps women of color at its core. Through the mission of this magazine, I've been able to interview educators, historians, authors, entrepreneurs, fashionistas, musicians, all who are hardworking women "doing the dang thang" day in and day out.

I've also made a deliberate and consistent decision to introduce readers to women of the past-trailblazers, "SHEros" whom we would be remiss if we failed to acknowledge their efforts, and sacrifices.

One such historical woman who receives ample attention is my "SHEro" Ida B. Wells, the fearless journalist, anti-lynching crusader, who's referred to as the "Princess of the Press."

My admiration of Wells led me to come in contact with Michelle Duster, the great-granddaughter of Wells. Without hesitation, I eagerly interviewed Michelle and the article appeared in the February 2013 digital issue of the magazine.

Michelle later invited me to contribute to a special book project on Michelle Obama, and I gladly accepted.

In September 2017, days before my wedding, I put the final touches on my essay for the book. *Michelle Obama's Impact on African American Women and Girls* was published in September 2018, and I planned an intimate book celebration with close friends and family at a local restaurant.

My cousin Keith was in attendance.

During my brief presentation at the event, I explained how this book came to be, described my connection with Michelle Duster, and read an excerpt from my essay titled "Michelle Obama: Marching to the Beat of her own Strengths and Defying Negative Stereotypes Along the Way."

Then it happened.

My cousin Keith raised his hand and asked:

"Cuz, I know you love the work of Ida B. Wells, but with all the work you've done so far with *ColorBlind* and now this essay, do you consider yourself an activist? I sense it in you."

I paused momentarily.

I can't remember my exact response, but I know it was something to the effect of: "Well cuz, I never really looked at myself that way."

But, I began to think: Perhaps I AM an activist because *ColorBlind* is the catalyst for my activism.

My publication has covered and discussed truthful and difficult stories; i.e., the release of Rochelle Riley's (a former award-winning columnist from the Detroit *Free Press*) book *The Burden: African American's and the Enduring Impact of Slavery*, the loss of the Queen of Soul—Aretha Franklin, reviews on epic gymnasts, Gabrielle Douglas and Simone Biles, #BringBackOurGirls, the work of Chicago artist Annie Lee, and, recently, an urging for my readers to read the work of Nikole Hannah-Jones regarding the *1619 Project* in *The New York Times Magazine.* In these ways, my magazine has upheld its triple E tagline "Enlighten, Encourage, Empower."

Future goals for the magazine include creating an online, interactive women's curriculum highlighting historical and contemporary women of color. This will educate, introduce and reinforce the work of these women and their acts of activism, which can be discussed in the classroom.

My magazine has taught me that activism goes beyond protests and picket signs; it means acting on whatever is right on large and small matters day after day.

So, I can rightfully say that each time I pick up my pen I'm participating in a form of activism. I never plan to put my pen down, even if I don't make a dime from it.

THE FIGHT AGAINST STEREOTYPES

Jennifer Brown Banks

"No one can do everything. But everybody can do something."
-Max Lucado

I once heard a comedian say, "If you want to hide your valuables from a Black person, tuck them between the pages of a book."

Though his joke held great hilarity for some, I wasn't laughing.

This plaguing stereotype continues to perpetuate the common myth that Black folks don't read. That we don't appreciate literature, culture and the arts. That is, with the exception of dancing and "Soul Train," of course.

Of all the lies and "stinkin' thinking" involving people of color, this was my Achilles heel.

Perhaps because I have always been an avid reader. My love affair with reading and writing began early. Growing up, my siblings and I had more books than toys.

Our home was filled with picture books, medical journals, autobiographies, and self-help bestsellers—hard covers, paper backs, big and small in a rainbow of colors.

My mom constantly drilled in us the importance of education, and how our ancestors died for the right for us to enjoy this privilege. And I never forgot that.

As the years evolved, I eventually became a reader, writer, award-winning poet, and arts enthusiast.

In 1994, I decided to change the literary landscape and perception of Black people by founding and organizing my own community-based arts organization in Chicago. Poets United to Advance the Arts was born. A local librarian (for whom we auditioned) agreed to provide a forum for us once a month.

Our mission? To increase arts awareness, promote advocacy, self-publish our own literature, and offer mutual support to kindred spirits. Our small but very active group even defied familiar "stereotypes": a curvaceous, cute female cop, a 6 foot 4 inch military veteran who was a gentle giant, an introvert who was a dynamic spoken word performer, and others with controversial views. Our colors? Black and white.

Fast forward…In June 2019, we celebrated twenty-five years of performing, publishing, and promoting the arts at universities, churches, galleries, private events. We have performed before audiences of all age groups, racial backgrounds, interests and industries. I was even honored at a banquet by Brainerd Community Development for my work.

When most people think of "activism," they think of courageous acts (like boycotts in Alabama), or the militant moves of the Black Panthers in the '60s.

But, sometimes, a "nudge" can be just as effective as a movement. Sometimes activism can simply be a raising of consciousness, a paradigm shift, or using one's platform to speak out against injustices.

Though I'll never qualify for a star on the Hollywood Walk of Fame, I'm proud that I have used my divine gifts for good. Words are an important legacy.

To quote John F. Kennedy: "One person can make a difference. And everyone should try."

TO BE SEEN AND HEARD

Tony Bradburn

I remember the moment when I was home on Dr. Martin Luther King Jr's holiday. Oprah was on, and she paid tribute to his work. As I sat there listening, she said that if it weren't for him, she wouldn't be able to have this show. As I heard those words, I admired her for her humility and also felt humbled myself. Both her words and his stimulated some thinking in me regarding how I could provide a tribute to him as well.

Being an English teacher at a high school of nearly 2,000 students (Rolling Meadows High School), I realized that I had multiple allies who would be willing to help. My prediction was right. After emailing them, they all were willing to gather and listen to the idea about adults sharing three stories about how race had affected them and to provide a challenge to students. On the day of the events, more than 700 students piled into the auditorium to listen to these stories. I didn't know that they were this hungry for this sort of conversation until they filled in all the seats, sat on stairs and in aisles, and gave standing ovations. I'm not sure I saw it all through my tears.

After this first year, we decided to turn it over to student voices. This was the first year of *The Cure*. The question that students had to answer (borrowed from Coldplay) related to racism. They were asked if they were "part of the cure or part of the disease?" Then, students were encouraged to perform a piece that would combat racism. The admission fee helped fund a scholarship for a racial activist.

Recently, one of my students shared that this work was my "punk manifesto." I smile just thinking of his words. Years later, a student who was in her thirties posted on social media:

> While I may not talk to many of my high school classmates in real life anymore, thanks to the beauty of Facebook I've kept up with the lives and opinions of many.

And y'all. I'm PROUD of you. You're good people and stand up for what's right and it's showing now more than ever.

I'm moved and strangely relieved because so many others I've met along the way have disappointed me SO much in what they've chosen to share and what matters to them. RMHS kids, keep being the good in this world. (I think our teachers had a lot to do with this—looking at you Tony Bradburn) #blacklivesmatter

This moved me because I didn't realize that my simple idea of sharing stories and inviting students to use their voices to combat racism would have such lasting effects. In fact, I wasn't even sure anyone would come!

At some level, though, this sort of work is simply part of my DNA. In fact, I brought it with me to Niles North High School in a suburb of Chicago. While there I was charged with creating one unified Humanities Department combining three separate departments: English, Social Studies, and Reading. With my counterpart from the neighboring school, we designed a new department, and in creating it, facilitated staff discussions that grappled with the question "How can one large department function better than we did as three separate departments?" With an elected team of teacher representatives, we discussed course offerings and many other facets of our functioning through a symbiotic lens and one of rigor and relevance.

While charting a path with adults for this new department, I also helped facilitate student forums. We addressed topics like equity, systemic racism, microaggressions, and Islamophobia. In these school-wide forums, I heard a recurring concern from students— why is our academic focus on "dead white males"?

All the while, my desire to make an impact led to the creation of a student group called *Notice!*—a mentoring group for Black males. My mentoring conversations with these students taught me that these young men had to activate epic proportions of perseverance and community in order to successfully navigate the academic world where the color of their skin made their stark minority status stand out. There was a need for a supportive space for the Black young men at Niles North for many reasons, but most importantly to build community and activate a sense of hope and unity between them. I assembled Black teachers, deans, paraprofessionals, security guards and administrators in order to outline goals and ensure strong role models. We came together with the students twice a month to break bread, discuss topics on an outlined agenda, and address other pressing matters as they surfaced.

These young men pulled at my heart strings multiple times. The first time was at our very first meeting. My simple goal was to let them know they mattered. I wasn't sure it was going to work. I wasn't sure students were going to show up. Even if they did show up, I wasn't sure they would return. But they did. After we had gathered, I told them what *Notice!* was about. Then, I explained that time and resources would be allocated to this group. Still nervous throughout this meeting, I followed up by asking the young men how often (if at all) they wanted to meet. When I heard a few students say "every day," my heart was filled with joy. The simple act of providing a space for Black men to eat and connect gave them a safe environment to relax and unwind.

Another one of my most cherished memories involved watching a student's emotions spill forth as he stood in front of nearly all the Black students (male and female) as he processed the murder of his mother and recounted it for all of us to feel. This space allowed a Black man to grieve.

Another time, I outfitted some graduating seniors with shirts and ties for prom and graduation. Seeing their smiles in the mirror after they learned to tie a tie will stay with me for decades. They went through this rite of passage together in a nurturing space.

We discussed literature, and they told me that even if the "n word" is in print, they don't want to hear it spoken out loud. I, then, had this conversation with the department. They knew they could trust me to share their voice.

In time, we had our last meeting where they decided to sit me down and tell me all the things they respected about me. They requested that I just listen and keep my mouth shut as they poured their affirmations into me. It wasn't until that moment that I realized what the space called *Notice!* had done for them. Paying attention to the concerns of these young men had a lasting effect on them.

Our school was in the midst of a significant transformation. We formed a Humanities Department, elevated discussions of equity, and created a safe space for Black students in *Notice!* As I listened to many voices during these transformative phases, I heard a subtle and consistent cry for change. I felt compelled to change our course offerings so that our curriculum would be stronger mirrors and windows for all our students.

In Social Studies, staff was compelled to offer new course offerings that reflected current student demographics to position our graduates for the world they were entering. Namely, we birthed two new courses: Asian American Studies and World Religions. These two courses came alive because not all our students and staff were able to see themselves in the movements, stories, and images of our curriculum. That is why schools exist — to serve the community in which we exist. Our school's Asian population rested at more than 30 %. However, we had no course that centered this demographic. So, we created one. In our newly created course, Asian American Studies, students wrestled with concepts of assimilation, the myth of the model minority, explored major immigration phases, visited Chinatown, and learned how Asian American identity development differs from the White majority. Our Asian students began to grasp words and concepts that had previously only landed as abstract feelings and unformed thoughts. Our non-Asian students became better equipped to support and love their Asian peers.

Our school families spoke more than ninety languages at home, and our family's religions mirrored our vast languages. In our newly created course, World Religions, students from different religious backgrounds stretched their understandings of current tensions in the Middle East and brought new awareness to terms like "jihad" and "religious cleansing."

By implementing two successful social science courses that deepened people's understanding of world religion and the Asian American experience, our students did not just learn facts. They learned how to understand each other better.

In English, we redesigned our offerings to incorporate more expansive topics including moral conflict, social justice, women and gender studies, and sports within American culture. We revamped our reading strands to provide more support for struggling students.

We encouraged the students to analyze the world around them and consider their own personal experiences when interpreting readings.

The result of these changes was significant growth in engagement, enthusiasm, and involvement of our students. Even the faculty became more invigorated and people flourished in this environment that allowed people to breathe and expand.

This experience gave me the tools and confidence to step into my new role as Principal of Roselle Middle School. I started advisory groups for parents and students. In fact, we created a fun tradition called Bagels with Bradburn, which gives the students the opportunity to share their ideas with me in an informal setting. We all work together to create curriculum, programs, and traditions that allow space for community voice and inclusion.

For me, the work of racial justice does not end at the classroom door. It continues into the community. If I can serve people in a way that helps them achieve their dreams, make the world safer, or bring justice to the underprivileged, I do. Life is too short for it to be spent oppressed.

ASHLEY JUDD GOES TO COLLEGE AT AGE 49

Laura Sweeney

When I think of sirens I think
cop cars, ambulances, Greek mythology,
but lately, I've been thinking about a tabloid
that read Ashley Judd wants to get her PhD
to end human trafficking. I read her book
All That is Bitter and Sweet, the black sheep

with a servant's heart, who made good
despite a troubled childhood. She crossed
the big stone gap of spinsterhood
even after the press poked fun of her
post-divorce bloat. Now it's her pink
bike and backpack they attack.

But Ashley Judd won't dignify that.
She is a global ambassador. Hollywood
prestige and glamour don't matter.
Now, its bodily integrity, gender equality,
combatting misogyny, she is after. And
I don't mean to put her on a pink pedestal,

but when some twenty-something asks
why I'm back in college, I will point
to a siren soaring towards her lofty fifty mind.
And when the dept. asks me to update
my accomplishments, I won't say I bought
a backpack and pink bike. I will say

if she can do it so can I. So *bon courage*
Ashley. I drink a toast to you and all
femme fatale-angels who embark
on a mid-life-changing odyssey.

Note: Ashley Judd enrolled in UC Berkeley, Public Policy, 2016

ACTIVISM

Unique Shaw-Smith and Chantae Still

The embodiment of a movement is not always public
Not always organized or even intentional in manner,
mind, body, or spirit
A collective inertia of morale manifesting in the day to
day lives of people who exist in places
where they are not always welcomed and embraced
Activism in academia is oftentimes a presence
Of being in the room and sharing a perspective that
would not otherwise be voiced
It is in the sharing of struggle, fable, or spirit-filled
songs to muster the courage to stand
Feet firmly planted in the face of Father Time
Whether real or imagined
The implications are not fabricated as many
livelihoods fall prey in the passing of midnight
hours
Stopped watch ticking time bombs of action
Erupt in command of voice, in plans of strategy, in
beating of shared heart drums
Passionate martyrs armed with resistance in the name
of solidarity
Justice is a revolutionary war

[i]
Clenched fist raised high with a doctorate degree in
hand
I wage battles against the mind in classrooms where
supremacy never sleeps
My activism occupies seats reserved for the privileged
majority

I challenge generationally imparted beliefs with
scholarship written by hands their ancestors
exploited
I require social justice-oriented assignments that
make them reflect on their role in the power
structures at play
I am versed in patriarchal gibberish and deconstruct
isms when I speak
I am the verb the colonizers wrote manuals of
instruction to quell
In the ranks of those they built ivory towers to defeat
I stumbled in and infiltrated the hallmark of elitist
construction
Assembly lines of production disrupted by an ebonic
speaking black womxn professor
I ain't your typical instructor
I brought my often imitated, never duplicated dearly
departed ancestors with me

[ii]
Enchanted Black women
Who bore life on a 200-pound bale of cotton
Spent hours cooking for the master with his tools only
to come home and create dishes out of
the belly of the beast
Something out of nothing
Became wise and knowledgeable when the world
considered her feeble-minded and dull
It is in the DNA of Black women
To supernaturally step outside of self, find fortitude,
and then pilgrimage across battlefields of
dictatorship, domination, and despotism
While simultaneously
Fighting against external forces of supremacy and
racism that attempt to give voice to doubt
To internalized hate
Nursing black woman back to loving images of their
diverse self

It is in the DNA of Black women
To stand up for human rights
Selfless in support for the cause of others while still
3/5ths whole in her own land
Reckless in pursuit of justice for all, knowing equity
frequently slips through her own hand
It is in my DNA to arrive the best version of myself
Kinked out with corn roll crowns creating spaces
for new images of young educated Black
women
Aware that my endeavor to get past the doctoral gates
and into the 2 percent is a precursor to
a war only Black women faculty can prepare me for
So I seek others with similar patterns of DNA
Enchanted Black women who occupy the academy
despite the blood, sweat, and tears shed
Carving a way for my critique

Key to writers: [i] Unique Shaw-Smith [ii] Chantae Still

MORE THAN MERELY KNOW

Marion Deutsche Cohen

I should do more than merely know.
More than merely write.
More than merely teach.
More than sign online petitions.
More than show up at demonstrations.
More than organize Poets against the Death Penalty
readings.

In early adolescence I swore, someday
I'd run out into the streets and scream
and scream again
have a public tantrum.

I'd also explain.
Never mind publishing, I'd be hard-copy.
Everyone would be in the streets.

I could use my math to prove to everyone.
I could prove my axioms to everyone.
I was sure I could prove or intuit to each and every one
what I merely knew.
But no matter how much we explain
no matter how much we prove
no matter how much we scream

we still also know.
We still have to know.

AFTERWORD

Trina Sotira

For many of us, protesting in helmets and bulletproof vests, battling against federal agents in military clothing — to secure human rights — is simply not an option. However, as the writers in this collection demonstrate, there are other paths toward change that have led — and will lead — to future action. While reading this book, I imagine you felt something — anger, sympathy, aggravation, or sorrow — but, my guess is you are not feeling rage. My guess is, since you took the time to engage with a writer, to listen to them reveal their struggles, you were able to find the human-ness in each story. In this highly polarized climate, when lifelong friends cut ties over Facebook arguments, I ask that we return to dialogue. Dialoging gives each participant a chance to hear the other side. Dialoging is more powerful than shouting, because, as psychotherapist Carl Rogers notes, we shut off communication when we feel threatened. Rubber bullets shout. Explosives scream. We only feed anger when we violently erupt. If we listen to each other, we can begin to value all voices. Listening says: I love you enough to hear you.

As many of the writers have shown, voicing opposition to social and political norms requires hope, tenacity, and endurance. But the impact is worth the effort. In a democratic society, everyone should have a voice in order to maintain a hopeful focus toward progress. Sarah Stitzlein's recent studies on hope suggest that "[h]oping engages in open-minded listening and collaboration; it brings people together rather than distances them." In concert with Stitzlein's studies on hope, I am reminded of educational theorist Paulo Freire's suggestion that hope "does not consist in crossing one's arms and waiting." I encourage all of you to uncross your arms and discuss issues that require change. A tweet is not a dialogue. A Facebook post is not a conversation. Now that we rely on video conferencing platforms to communicate, we need to meet each other at the virtual table to listen, dialogue, and think critically about how we can effectively change programs and policies to advance human rights.

Thank you for taking the time to hear the talented writers and activists in *Impact: Personal Portraits of Activism*. I hope they inspired you to effect change for something you care about—*your* human rights—*your* democratic society—so you too can positively impact *our* future. Freire reminds us: "Only by abolishing the situation of oppression is it possible to restore the love which that situation made possible. If I do not love the world—if I do not love life—if I do not love people—I cannot enter a dialogue." Thank you for showing your love for a just society by reading this book. Please spread love by engaging in conversations with others. Take the necessary footsteps toward future action.

CONTRIBUTORS

Dee Allen. is an African-Italian performance poet based in Oakland, California. He has been active on the creative writing & Spoken Word tips since the early 1990s. Author of five books (*Boneyard, Unwritten Law, Stormwater* and *Skeletal Black*, all from POOR Press; and his newest from Conviction 2 Change Publishing, *Elohi Unitsi*) and twenty-four anthology appearances, including *Your Golden Sun Still Shines, Rise, Extreme, The Land Lives Forever* and *Civil Liberties United*, edited by Shizué Seigel under his figurative belt so far.

Annette M. Alston is an award-winning writer and author of *Harriet Tubman for Beginners*. She is a retired Newark Public Schools teacher and activist. She is a member of the People's Organization for Progress, The Alliance for Newark Public Schools, Greater Life Ministries, The Essex Civic Association chapter of the National Council of Negro Women (NCNW), the Newark NAACP, and St. John #12 Chapter of the Order of Eastern Stars.

Jennifer Brown Banks is an award-winning poet, writer and columnist. Her work has been published in online and print publications which include: *Today's Black Woman* magazine, *Being Single, Chicago Sun-Times* and the *Final Call*. She is a former board member of Chicago Writers Association.

Brian C. Billings is an associate professor of drama and English at Texas A&M University-Texarkana and the general editor for *Aquila Review*. He wrote *Any Other Name* to bring attention to the many student attempts made in his region to remove Confederate statues and change controversial school names.

Aila Alvina Boyd is a Virginia-based writer, educator, and multiple award-winning print journalist. She holds undergraduate degrees in theatre and media studies from Radford University and a terminal graduate degree in writing from Lindenwood University. She serves on the Board of Directors of OutChristian, a national LGBTQ Christian organization.

Tony Bradburn, educator and advocate, pursues justice in ways that are almost always measurable, even if he cannot predict it in the moment. Expanding on this passion, he most recently started a community Facebook group that grew to more than 400 members by its one-week anniversary. Find it at "Activists for Racial Equity (Crystal Lake and Surrounding Community)." Knowing Jesus was lynched inspires his support of the underprivileged.

Lisa Braxton is an essayist, short story writer, and Emmy-nominated former television journalist. She is a Kimbilio fellow, a national residency for fiction writers, and a book reviewer. Her debut novel, *The Talking Drum*, was published by Inanna Publications in May 2020. Her website: lisabraxton.com. Twitter: @LisaReidbraxton

A. J. Chilson was born in Dallas, Texas in 1984. He began to write poetry as a teenager. Since then, Chilson has published books of poetry as well as children's stories. He currently lives in Princeton, Texas.

Deirdre L. Clawson, a careful observer, has been writing since she was a child. Currently she is working on a novel detailing the riveting diaspora of the Sampson family. When asked what she hopes to accomplish with her writing, Deirdre says, "I want to bring the world to a better understanding of itself." Previously attending the Abrie Writing Center in France and the Norman Mailer Writers Colony in New York City, Deirdre is now mainly writing from her Maryland home. Deirdre has studied writing at Wayne State University and is employed full time as a teacher where she has been awarded for her contributions for teaching cultural diversity.

Marion Deutsche Cohen is the author of thirty-one collections of poetry or memoir; her latest poetry collections are *The Essence of Seventh Grade: A Kind of Autobiography* (Alien Buddha Press), *The*

Project of Being Alive (New Plains Press, AL), and *The Discontinuity at the Waistline: My #MeToo Poems* (Rhythm and Bones Press, PA). She is also the author of two controversial memoirs about spousal chronic illness, a trilogy diary of late-pregnancy loss, and *Crossing the Equal Sign* about the experience of mathematics. She teaches a course she developed, Mathematics in Literature, at Drexel University, as well as a new course, Societal Issues on the College Campus. Other interests are classical piano, singing, Scrabble, thrift-shopping, four grown children, and five grands, another on the way. Her website is marioncohen.net.

Richard Downing has received the Nuclear Age Peace Foundation's Peace Poetry Prize, Writecorner Press Editor's Award, New Delta Review's Matt Clark Prize, and Solstice Literary Magazine's Editor's Award. He holds a PhD in English and is a co-founder of both the Florida Peace Action Network and Save Our Nature Coast.

Terri Elders, LCSW, a lifelong writer and editor, has contributed to over 130 anthologies. After a quarter-century odyssey, including a decade overseas with the Peace Corps, five years ago she finally returned to her native California, where she lives not far from her beloved Pacific Ocean. Blog: atouchoftarragon.blogspot.com

Dr. Linda L. Elman taught Spanish in the public schools for twenty-eight years, followed by fifteen years at DePauw University in Indiana. After being unlawfully fired for union activities, she fought to win her job back. She is blessed with two granddaughters and two grandsons.

Clara B. Freeman, born and raised in Mississippi, is an activist, poet, author, and former nurse, currently residing in the Midwest. Her work appears on websites, in newspapers, magazines and several anthologies, including *When One Door Closes, Reflections from Women on Life's Turning Points, Michelle Obama's Impact on African American Women and Girls, Black Lives Have Always Mattered, The Book of Hope,* and *Fiction International 51 World in Pain*. Clara's book, *Unleash Your Pearls Empowering Women's Voices* (2017), is available on Amazon.com. For more of her work, visit her weblog at http://wisewoman2.wordpress.com and follow her on Twitter @C50something.

CMarie Fuhrman is the author of *Camped Beneath the Dam: Poems* (Floodgate 2020) and co-editor of *Native Voices* (Tupelo 2019). She has published poetry and nonfiction in multiple journals including *High Desert Journal, Yellow Medicine Review, Cutthroat, a Journal of the Arts, Whitefish Review, Broadsided Press, Taos Journal of Poetry and Art,* as well as several anthologies. CMarie is a 2019 graduate of the University of Idaho's MFA program, a regular columnist for *Inlander,* and an editorial team member for Broadsided Press and nonfiction editor for *High Desert Journal.* CMarie resides in the mountains of West Central Idaho.

Stephanie J. Gates is an educator, writer and activist using her passion for social justice and equity to fuel her work both inside and outside of the classroom. She has developed and facilitated workshops nationally on issues of equity, and is most proud of her work against colorism. She created *Pretty is Me/Handsome I Am Day,* an annual event celebrating the diversity of beauty instead of a one-size-fits-all. Stephanie's work is featured in *Shifts: An Anthology of Women's Growth Through Change*, as well as a host of other anthologies and online publications.

Sharron Goodman-Hill is an instructor of Mass Communications at Rust College, and hosts "A Little Bit of Heaven" weekday mornings for WURC in Holly Springs, Mississippi. Additionally, she serves as host and producer of *Straight Talk Live*, a weekly public affairs program on WURC. She is the founder of the annual Ida B. Wells Symposium, an event that honors its namesake for the contributions Wells made in journalism and civil rights.

Alexandra Grabbe is the author of *Wellfleet, An Insider's Guide to Cape Cod's Trendiest Town.* For ten years she wrote a blog about living green on Cape Cod. Her recent work has appeared in *The Washington Post, Better After Fifty,* and the *Compassion Anthology.* More can be found at alexandragrabbe.com.

Sandra (Sandy) Hall, MSW, MA - CEO of Memory Lane Publishers is a writer, social worker, and restorative justice (RJ) practitioner. She facilitates workshops for youth and adults on grief and loss. She has been fighting for justice for over forty years individually, as a member of the Chicago Association of Black Social Workers, and as an RJ practitioner for the last fifteen years. Her book, *Fathers R Special Too, Celebrating Daddy N'em*, released June 2020, is her eighth publication. (www.celebr8lifedaily.com)

Judy Hogan, co-editor of *Hyperion: A Poetry Journal* (1970-81), founding editor of Carolina Wren Press (1976-91) is a creative writing teacher and activist. Her newest mystery, *Don't Frack Here*, is her twelfth. The Sallie Bingham Center for Women's History and Culture at Duke University has her papers. She chairs the fight against dumping coal ash in Moncure, NC.

Hunter Liguore is an award-winning author whose work promotes understanding our shared humanity through compassion. She teaches social justice writing at Lesley University in Cambridge. Follow her @skytale_Writer or hunterliguore.org.

Chad W. Lutz is a non-binary writer born in Akron, Ohio in 1986 and raised in the neighboring suburb of Stow. They graduated from Kent State University with their BA in English in 2008 and from Mills College in Oakland, California, with their MFA in Creative Writing in 2018.

Jarrett Mazza is a graduate of Goddard College's MFA in Creative Writing Program, as well as The Humber School For Writers. He has taught writing courses and has had stories published online in *GNU Journal, Bewildering Stories, Trembling With Fear, Aphelion,* Silver Empire, *Scarlet Leaf Review, Toronto Prose Mill,* and Zimbell House Publishing. He will also be featured in forthcoming anthologies titled *Mother's Ghost Grim* and *The Killer Collection Anthology*, both published by NBH Publishers, and another by Dragon Soul Press. Jarrett received an Honorable Mention for the Freda Walton Award for Fiction by the Short Works Prize at the Hamilton Public Library. He lives in Hamilton, Ontario. Twitter @JarrettMazza

Greta McClain's essay, "The Birth of Healing and Activism," explains how rape and #MeToo led to a rebirth of purpose and confidence, as well as her commitment to supporting fellow sexual assault survivors in her community. As a freelance writer, Greta has published several editorials in *The Tennessean* newspaper, an essay in *The Contributor* newspaper, and numerous news articles through Digital Journal.

Erin Goseer Mitchell, a native Georgian, recently moved back to Atlanta after living in Chicago for 60 years. She was an educator in the Chicago Public Schools system for 38 years. After her retirement, a passion for writing emerged. She began writing what grew into her first book, *Born Colored: Life Before Bloody Sunday*. Her second book, *From Colored to Black,* was published in 2016. She is proud of her two daughters and three grandsons.

Carole Ann Moleti is a nurse-midwife and family nurse practitioner who lives and works in New York City. She specializes in the care of women and families at high psychosocial risk. Excerpts of Carole's memoirs, *Someday I'm Going to Write A Book: Diary of An Urban Missionary* and *Karma, Kickbacks and Kids* have been published in a variety of literary venues including the acclaimed *Shifts Anthology*, *Not Your Mother's Books: On Being a Woman* and *On Being a Mother*, *This Path,* and *Thanksgiving to Christmas: A Quilt of Holidays.* She won the *Oasis Journal* award for best nonfiction in 2009. Carole also writes science fiction and fantasy because walking through walls is less painful than running into them.

Rita Moe's poetry has appeared in *Water~Stone*, *Poet Lore*, *Slipstream* and other literary journals. She is the author of two poetry chapbooks, *Sins & Disciplines* and *Findley Place; A Street, a Ballpark, a Neighborhood*. She has two grown sons and lives with her husband in Roseville, Minnesota.

Naida Mujkic, PhD, has published in literary journals and anthologies around the world. So far, she has published five books of poetry and one book of lyrical prose. She has participated in several international poetry and literature festivals.

Allene Nichols is a teacher and a writer who also enjoys photography and backpacking. Her poetry has appeared in many journals and anthologies, including *Veils, Halos & Shackles, Lifting the Sky, Southwestern Haiku and Haiga,* and *Impossible Archetype.* Her plays have been performed throughout the United States.

Leah Olajide has worked in the field of communication/ journalism since 2011 and has loved writing since she was eleven years old. She has worked at nonprofits in Detroit and Dearborn, using her writing and editing skills in a variety of assignments. Some of Olajide's more recent work includes a published essay in the book *Michelle Obama's Impact on African American Women and Girls.* She is also pursuing a master's degree in Communication/Journalism to teach college students and offer them internships via her publication, *ColorBlind Magazine.*

Keith A. Raymond, MD is a family and emergency physician who practiced in eight countries and four languages. He currently lives in Austria. When not volunteering his medical skills, he is writing or lecturing. He has multiple medical citations, along with publications in *Flash Fiction Magazine, The Grief Diaries, The Examined Life Journal, The Satirist, Chicago Literati, Blood Moon Rising, Frontier Tales Magazine,* and in the Zimbell House Publishing Sci Fi anthology *Sanctuary,* among others.

Leslie Penelope Recht is a lifelong resident of Chicago with a BA from the University of Chicago and a law degree from Chicago-Kent College of Law. Her volunteer activities cover diverse areas. She is a past president of The Cliff Dwellers arts club and a strong supporter of historic preservation.

Jacqueline Ruegg is a British poet, writer and educator currently living in Massachusetts. "Day One" was inspired by her experience of, and attempt to process, the aftermath of the 2016 election and the importance of activism in defending humans and human rights.

Terry Sanville lives in San Luis Obispo, California with his artist-poet wife and two plump cats. His stories have been accepted more than 360 times by journals and anthologies. Two of his stories have been nominated for the Pushcart Prize and one for inclusion in the Best of the Net Anthology. Terry is a retired urban planner and an accomplished jazz and blues guitarist.

Gerard Sarnat is a poet, physician, executive, academic and social activist. Gerry's built and staffed homeless and prison clinics, plus been a Stanford professor and healthcare CEO. Currently he is devoting energy/resources to work with internationally known and recognized leaders addressing climate change justice. Married since 1969, he has three children and six grandsons.

Anjana Satpathy lives and works in Bangalore, India. She believes in enjoying the small, simple moments in life and tries to capture the beauty of those moments in words. Find her online at flowersbutterflies.home.blog or follow her on Instagram @anjanasatpathy.

Anne Farrer Scott's work has appeared in *The New York Times*, *The Examined Life*, *Hungry Mind Review*, *Family Circle*, *Minnesota Monthly*, and other publications. She received an SCBWI Work-in-Progress Nonfiction Award, a Loft-McKnight Award, an Artist's Assistance Award from the Minnesota State Arts Board, and a First Place, Best News Story, from the Iowa Newspaper Foundation. She worked for several Iowa newspapers and for many years led a writing workshop at an Iowa medium security prison. She strives and struggles to write (hopefully) creative nonfiction.

Judy Seldin-Cohen co-authored *Recharging Judaism: How Civic Engagement is Good for Synagogues, Jews, & America*, a Myra H. Kraft Award finalist for the National Jewish Book Awards (Schindler and Seldin-Cohen, CCAR Press, 2018). She chairs a $26 million public-private housing endowment and speaks at synagogues and other community forums. Meet her at judyseldincohen.com.

Unique R. Shaw-Smith has a PhD in Sociology with an emphasis in Criminology. She describes herself as a Black mother scholar activist poet.

Chantae Still is a fourth-year doctoral candidate in the Curriculum Instruction Adult Education program at the University of South Florida in Tampa, Florida. She describes herself as a Black novice qualitative researcher. Twitter: @D_Chantae

Patti Capel Swartz has published a number of both academic and literary essays and poetry. She also wrote and directed several oral history plays about the eastern Ohio Valley region of Appalachian Ohio. Swartz taught creative writing, literature, composition, and honors classes at Kent State University East Liverpool. She is currently a retired faculty member of Kent State.

Laura Sweeney facilitates Writers for Life in central Iowa. She represented the Iowa Arts Council at the First International Teaching Artists Conference in Olso, Norway. She has published poems in over fifty journals, including Canada, Britain, and China. Her recent awards include a scholarship to attend the 2019 Sewanee Writers' Conference.

Marianne Taylor, Poet Laureate of Mount Vernon, IA, is the recipient of several prizes and awards for her work, which appears widely in national journals and anthologies. She also writes and directs plays, teaches literature and creative writing at Kirkwood Community College, and has served on her city council and numerous theatre, arts, and education boards.

Uzomah Ugwu is an emerging poet and writer. She is a political, social and cultural activist. Her core focus is on human rights, mental health, animal rights, and rights of LGBTQ persons. Her work has been featured in *Prelude Magazine, Tuck Magazine* and *Wild Word*, the *Angel City Review, Voice of Eve, Scarlet Leaf Review*, and more.

Susan M. Winstead has been published in newspapers, magazines and anthologies and she has won several writing awards. She is past summer program chair, program chair, and president of Off Campus Writers' Workshop. She currently serves as a board member for Jane's Story Press Foundation. She is a graduate of Western Illinois University where she also received an ROTC commission and served on active duty in the U.S. Army.

EDITORS

Michelle Duster is a writer, professor, public historian, and champion of racial and gender equity. She wrote *Ida B the Queen*; co-wrote the popular children's history book, *Tate and His Historic Dream*; co-edited *Michelle Obama's Impact on African American Women and Girls*; and edited two books that include the writings of her great-grandmother, Ida B. Wells. She has written articles for *TIME, Essence, Huffington Post, Teen Vogue,* and *The North Star.* Her advocacy has led to street names, monuments, historical markers, and other public history projects that highlight women and African Americans.

Trina Sotira is an Associate Professor of English/Creative Writing. A writer grounded in social justice issues, Trina is the author of the YA novel *In Her Skin: Growing Up Trans* and is finishing a doctorate in curriculum leadership, with a proposed dissertation in Critical Race Theory. Trina served as the advisor of the college literary journal *The Prairie Light Review,* where her students won the American Scholastic Press Association's First Place Magazine award four consecutive years during her tenure. She has spoken at numerous academic and literary conferences, including the Association for the Study of African American Life and History, Illinois Reading Council, and the Illinois Society of Children's Book Writers and Illustrators. Her work has been published in *The Poeming Pigeon, Emerge Literary Journal,* and *WOW! Women on Writing.*

Impact: Personal Portraits of Activism is Michelle and Trina's second collaboration under MuseWrite Press. Their first project, *Shifts: An Anthology of Women's Growth Through Change,* is an Indie Book Award and USA Best Book Award finalist in the women's issues category.

DISCUSSION QUESTIONS

for *Impact: Personal Portraits of Activism*

1. What is the overarching theme of the book? How are the stories connected?

2. Describe which issues or ideas the writers explore and which remain especially memorable.

3. What new information did you learn about people who have had different experiences or cultural backgrounds? How has your perspective changed about something that you originally weren't familiar with?

4. Which issues addressed in the book affect your life the most? Did the writers capture your feelings or experiences? What are the similarities and differences between your experiences and those of the writers?

5. What are the implications for the future? Are there long- or short-term consequences to the issues raised in the book? Are they positive or negative? Affirming or frightening? Consider a comparison between the past, present, and future.

6. Did you find any of the pieces to be controversial? If so why? Explain how a specific piece might incite disdain or anger, or even cause readers to feel uncomfortable. Did the writer's perspective help you think about something in a different way?

7. Talk about pieces that struck you as significant — or interesting, profound, amusing, illuminating, disturbing, or sad. What was memorable?

8. What issues in your community need attention? Based on other activists' and writers' experiences in *Impact*, how will you begin to spark change? What are the steps you will take to start a dialogue about this issue?

Writing Prompt

9. What issues/topics do you feel could have been addressed in a different way? What would you add to the conversation? Create a fiction or creative nonfiction story, poem, or essay about this topic. You might respond to one of the writers, or write the piece from your own perspective to let your voice be heard. Feel free to e-mail the editors of *Impact* with a copy of your writing from this prompt. MuseWrite Press could choose your work for either their website or future publications. (Communication will be established before any work is printed.)

For further insight, or to contact one of the book's contributors or editors, email MuseWrite Press at MuseWriteCommunity@yahoo.com.

Made in the USA
Middletown, DE
07 November 2020